MOVING TO ONLINE

Ernest W. Brewer
Jacquelyn O. DeJonge
Vickie J. Stout

MOVING TO ONLINE

Making
the
Transition
From
Traditional
Instruction and
Communication Strategies

CORWIN PRESS, INC.
A Sage Publications Company
Thousand Oaks, California

For information:

Corwin Press, Inc.
A Sage Publications Company
2455 Teller Road
Thousand Oaks, California 91320
E-mail: order@corwinpress.com

Sage Publications Ltd.
6 Bonhill Street
London EC2A 4PU
United Kingdom

Sage Publications India Pvt. Ltd.
M-32 Market
Greater Kailash I
New Delhi 110 048 India

Printed in the United States of America

Library of Congress Cataloging-in-Publication Data

Brewer, Ernest W.
    Moving to online: Making the transition from traditional instruction and
communication strategies / by Ernest W. Brewer, Jacquelyn O. DeJonge,
and Vickie J. Stout.
        p. cm.
    Includes bibliographical references and index.
    ISBN 0-7619-7787-2 (cloth: alk. paper)   ISBN 0-7619-7788-0 (pbk.: alk. paper)
    1. Computer-assisted instruction. 2. Adult education.
3. Distance education. I. DeJonge,
Jacquelyn O. II. Stout, Vickie J. III. Title
LB1028.5 .B673 2001
371.33'4—dc21   00-065946

This book is printed on acid-free paper.

01   02   03   04   05   06   10   9   8   7   6   5   4   3   2   1

Corwin Editorial Assistant:	Kylee Liegl
Production Editor:	Nevair Kabakian
Editorial Assistant:	Kathryn Journey
Cover Designer:	Tracy E. Miller

TABLE OF CONTENTS

PART IV APPLICATION METHODS   *145*

Chapter 10 *Application Method: Role-Playing*   *147*

ACKNOWLEDGMENTS

The authors acknowledge The University of Tennessee, the College of Human Ecology, and the Department of Human Resource Development, and the HRD students who have learned *from* and continue to learn lessons *about* how people learn and build relationships from a distance. We also recognized the DIMS team of faculty for bravely sharing in the process of learning new ways to communicate and effectively teach online.

We thank personnel at Corwin Press and Sage Publications for their helpful tips in manuscript preparation and for final editing. Thanks especially go to Nevair Kabakian, Production Editor, and to Robb Clouse, Acquistions Editor, for their patience and support.

Thanks to The Stock Market for their photo images which are royalty-free stock photography and also to the Blackboard, Inc., for their online computer frame design that helps illustrate teaching online.

Finally, we express our appreciation to our families for their support as we completed this project.

Ernest W. Brewer
Jacquelyn O. DeJonge
Vickie J. Stout

ABOUT THE AUTHORS

Ernest W. Brewer is a Professor in the Department of Human Resource Development at The University of Tennessee (UT). In addition, he is the Principal Investigator/Director of Federal Programs and he has just completed a two-year appointment as Department Head of the Department of Child and Family Studies. Dr. Brewer has authored or co-authored a variety of books and articles. *Foundations of Workforce Education: Historical, Philosophical, and Theoretical Applications* (2000, Kendall/Hunt Publishers), *Finding Funding: Grantwriting and Project Implementation* (1998, Corwin Press), *Promising Practices* (1999, Holcomb Hathaway Publishers), and *Characteristics, Skills, and Strategies of the Ideal Educator* (2000, Pearson Education) are four of his recent books. He is completing an additional two books at this time. He is also Editor of the *Journal of Educational Opportunity* and Editor of *International Journal of Vocational Education and Training*.

Several years ago, Dr. Brewer was presented with the Outstanding Excellence in Distance Education Award in Teaching. In addition to being a teacher [professor], he is a Certified Professional Counselor (PC) and is certified as a high school counselor.

Jacquelyn O. DeJonge is a Professor in the Department of Human Resource Development at The University of Tennessee (UT). Prior to joining this department in 1998 she held academic administrative postions at UT. She served as Dean of the College of Human Ecology and as a department head for a total of 20 years. She has been recognized for her contributions to higher education and has consulted with national and international organizations. She has received Professional Achievement Awards from Michigan State University and Iowa State University, where she received her Masters and Ph.D. degrees, respectively. The YWCA has recognized her with the Tribute to Women Education Award in 1992. She has consulted with professional organizations on strategic planning. These organizations include the Intrenational Textile and Apparel Association;

Seoul National University, Korea; Kent State University, and others. She participated in a Fulbright Exchange Agreement with Helwan University in Cairo, Egypt. She has developed and taught online courses at UT since 1998. These HRD courses were at both the undergraduate and graduate level.

Vickie J. Stout is an Associate Professor in the Department of Human Resource Development (HRD) at The University of Tennessee (UT). With more than 25 years' experience in the field of human resouce development, she has provided training, program development, and technial assistance consulting for organizations such as Digital Equipment Corporation, AT&T, and Allied Signal. Her teaching responsibilities at UT include teacher education and graduate and undergraduate instruction in Business Education and Marketing Education. Dr. Stout has co-authored three other books and a variety of articles. From 1997-99 she served as Project Coordinator for the HRD Diversified Instructional Modality Sytems (DIMS) Team, which was responsible for the initial design, development, and delivery of HRD's undergraduate degree program core courses. Since 1998 she has taught online coureses at both the undergraduate and graduate level. She also serves as a member of the curriculum development committee for a federally-funded Learning Anytime Anywhere Partnership (LAAP) Grant and on the Planning Committee for the UT Sytem's New College, an inter-institutional electronic campus which will provide electronic learning opportunities.

DEDICATION

This book is dedicated to the inspired individuals and resourceful institutions that pioneered the development of Web-based technologies, as well as to the creative spirits who will undoubtedly launch those same technologies into a future we can only dream of today.

PART I
GENERAL OVERVIEW OF ONLINE INSTRUCTION

CHAPTER 1
GENERAL INFORMATION

CHAPTER 2
ONLINE LEARNING: A HISTORICAL PERSPECTIVE

CHAPTER 3
MOVING FROM TRADITIONAL CLASSROOM INSTRUCTION TO ONLINE INSTRUCTION

CHAPTER 4
FACILITATING ONLINE LEARNING

CHAPTER 1

GENERAL INFORMATION

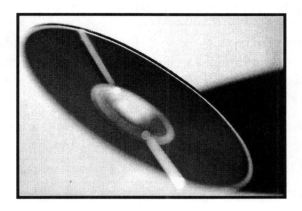

Whether you are a secondary or postsecondary teacher, a trainer, a seminar leader, or a team leader designated to bring an idea to the executive committee, this book is for you. Any of these information presentation techniques may be appropriate for a given learning session—depending on the topic.

You may ask, "How can I use these techniques in my instruction?" Some online users may want to consider the techniques, select one to experiment with, and, after the session, evaluate themselves on their effectiveness. We do not pretend to exhaust the range of possibilities with these techniques. Rather, we focus on several examples that we have come to value for their versatility and effectiveness while teaching at a university and making presentations or conducting workshops in the business community that incorporate some online learning experiences.

The contents of each chapter will be of considerable value to individuals who are preparing for teaching online at any level of instruction—middle school, high school, or college—or for training individuals in the work environment. Many experienced teachers and trainers may also find that the various techniques provide criteria for technical decisions they must make regarding classroom instruction. An effort has been made to provide a general and, to some extent, conceptual analysis of practices in teaching and presenting online. Our intention and hope is that the book will provide trainers, teachers, and others concerned with instruction some general guidelines for thinking about instructional practice. Throughout the book, the choice of techniques does not dictate what the classroom practitioner ought to do. Peculiarities in teaching situations vary so widely that it seems ill advised to attempt to prescribe practices that should be universally and literally implemented.

One aspect of an online presenter's work is to exercise skill in judgment and apply his or her specialized knowledge to fashion the specifics of the teaching practice.

What Are Teaching and Learning?

The teacher teaching online performs many tasks during the period of a course or training session. Although some of those activities take place in the absence of participants or students, teaching occurs when the online practitioner directly or indirectly interacts with one or more participants online, with the intent that the participants learn from the encounter. The teacher or trainer directs participants to do certain things with the expectation that they will learn from the activity. Some educational scholars compare teaching and learning to buying and selling. The analogy of teaching and selling is a coordinate concept, but the analogy of learning and buying is not. Nevertheless, one can conclude that selling is possible only if there are buyers. Similarly, one cannot teach unless another is receiving instruction and, hopefully, learning.

The Basic Laws of Learning

The laws of learning fall into two main categories: primary and secondary. The primary laws consist of the *law of readiness, law of exercise* or repetition (including drill and practice), and *law of effect*. The three secondary laws are the *laws of primacy, recency,* and *intensity*. Malone (1991) noted that educational pioneers such as Edward Lee Thorndike and John Broadus Watson refer to other laws as well. For example, there are the *laws of set or attitude, associative shifting,* and *analogy.*

With regard to the primary laws, the *law of readiness* informs the classroom practitioner that when a participant is ready to learn and that person can connect experiences he or she has had in the past with the knowledge to be acquired, optimal learning may result. Readiness implies that a person is eager to learn what is being presented or addressed in the workshop. Participants typically learn with greater facility when they are able to associate some of their past experiences with new material. They also must be interested and motivated in order to learn. This eagerness must precede the introduction of content. The online practitioner often can establish this state of readiness by helping participants see the need to learn or the value of what is to be presented. "Involving adults in clarifying their own ambiguous needs and in defining clear learning needs is acknowledged as one of the most important aspects of adult learning" (Knowles, 1990, cited in MacKeracher, 1997, p.79).

The second primary law, the *law of exercise,* informs educators of the importance of practice and repetition. Ordinarily, participants must practice what they are learning if they are to remember it. It is most important that participants be given opportunities to practice or repeat the skills and knowledge they are expected to retain. Learners can be assisted in developing skills through feedback that is specific, descriptive, and objective.

The final primary law is the *law of effect,* which Mazur (1990) references in his book. This law suggests that learning and retention are strengthened when the participant receives pleasure from the learning activity. Learning is weakened if participants experience displeasure with the activity. It is essential that individuals experience the content in a meaningful way and that they receive pleasure and satisfaction from the learning activities being presented. Presenters and teachers must therefore not only present material in such a manner as to engage the interest of participants, they must also avoid procedures that would be counterproductive. For example, if someone consistently interacts with the material in such a way that they experience failure, that individual will become far less interested in that particular learning experience. This also relates to the law of readiness, because in order to interact productively with the material, the learner must be in a state of readiness. Often learners need a variety of activities for interacting with the same information or practicing a set of skills. Variety can be a tremendous aid not only for avoiding boredom but also for broadening conceptual understanding.

The secondary laws of primacy and recency are somewhat self-explanatory. For example, the *law of primacy* reminds us of the importance of first impressions. Typically, what is learned at the beginning of a session is remembered best. Often, learning that occurs at the end is also retained well. The middle segment of a presentation will have less impact unless the presenter or teacher finds a way to highlight that segment in the learner's memory. The *law of recency* suggests that the stronger the connection, the more intense the learning will be between the stimuli and the response.

The *law of recency* should be considered throughout the learning process. When considering the material or skill that is most important, one must select carefully the activities and their timing. Otherwise, the result may be that basic information or other learning does not make optimum impact on participants. The main part of a learning experience ideally will be highlighted in the memories of learners through the strategic selection and timing of activities. One aid for this may be found in another of the secondary laws, the *law of intensity.*

In working with the *law of intensity*, the classroom practitioner attempts to make the experience vivid and exciting. Scintillating activities are certainly more likely to be retained than mundane ones. At times, this presents a special challenge, because the educator also must remember the primary law dealing with the need for exercise, or repetition.

As mentioned earlier, the educational scholars Thorndike and Watson alluded to other laws, such as the *law of set or attitude.* An example of working with this law is that competent instructors begin the instruction with an anticipatory set—that is, a brief activity designed to gain participants' attention and get them focused on the topic. This focus must be a matter of both mind and attitude. Thorndike's (1905) *law of associative shifting* refers to a personal and cultural predisposition to behave in a particular way in a particular situation. There is also the *law of analogy,* which considers transfer of successful responses from one environment to another.

Another law alluded to by Thorndike is the *law of multiple responses.* This law states that if one response does not solve a problem, another response will be tried. Facilitators can encourage learners to practice this law by providing a nonthreatening environment. Although some of these concepts are better understood and may have greater applicability in a given setting than others, the educator will be well advised to adhere to these general principles or laws when preparing for each learning session.

Teaching in the Cognitive, Affective, and Psychomotor Domains

Two major handbooks provide extensive information on these taxonomies. Bloom, Englehart, Furst, Hill, & Krathwohl's (1956) *Taxonomy of Educational Objectives—Handbook I* focuses on the cognitive domain. Krathwohl, Bloom, and Masia's (1964) *Taxonomy of Educational Objectives—Handbook II* followed later and provides detailed information on the affective domain. Simpson (1972) classifies the major classifications of the psychomotor domain that currently are used extensively by classroom practitioners.

Most educators and trainers are familiar with Bloom's (1976) *Taxonomy of Critical Thinking Skills.* Hunter (1990) noted that Bloom separated cognition into six levels. Bloom's *cogitive domain* classification, listed from lowest level to highest, includes

✗ **Knowledge**—receiving information. Examples: learning how many people inhabit a specified area; memorizing the Gettysburg Address.

✗ **Comprehension**—learning the concept of multiplication as a process of rapid addition; learning the meaning of the concepts stated in the Preamble to the U.S. Constitution.

✗ **Application**—computing mathematical problems (3x14); completing a simple chemistry lab experiment after seeing a demonstration.

✗ **Analysis**—separating the whole into parts; determining cause-effect relationships.

✗ **Synthesis**—bringing together information from different sources on a specified topic to create a fuller understanding of the topic; solving a mystery after gathering pertinent data and analyzing it.

✗ **Evaluation**—determining the strengths and weaknesses of a program; completing a book review in which the relative merits of the book are discussed.

Many of these thinking skills are self-explanatory. One who is present at a lecture or a panel discussion, for example, first receives and then hopefully comprehends the information. In such educational settings, there may be little opportunity to think at a higher level because the flow of information does not allow for it. Strategies such as role-playing, inquiry, and case study are slower in pace and require much more sophisticated thought processes. For example, in a case study the participants must apply their knowledge to the given study as they seek a solution to the problem. In doing so, they analyze the facts and synthesize the given information with (or integrate it into) their prior knowledge. Participants likely will propose numerous alternatives, evaluate the possibilities, and select the one that their analysis indicates is the best answer to the problem. As noted on the Table 1.2 on page 25, those strategies that require complex thinking are generally conducted in group settings. When teaching online to a large group, individuals can be broken down into smaller groups to facilitate interaction and address a variety levels of learning. Strategies such as the case study, the inquiry method, and questioning are most effective when the size of the group permits active involvement of everyone.

Another way to approach cognitive learning has been presented by Miller (1991). According to Miller, the levels contained within Bloom's taxonomy may be approached either analytically or holistically. Analytical thinking breaks down information into small pieces and examines them in a systematic, inductive fashion, whereas holistic thinking involves deductively looking for relationships within "the big picture," with less attention to detail. Although most learners at times make use of each style, most also have a preferred style.

Web-based learning supports cognitive skills development. Cognitive skills involve every level of Bloom's taxonomy, and many web-based activities, including interaction with other learners, can be used to enhance cognitive learning.

Henson (1996) defines **affective domain** as the part of "human learning that involves changes in interests, attitudes, and values" (p. 57). Krathwohl et al. (1964) classified the affective domain into five major categories—receiving, responding, valuing, organizing, and characterizing. The affective domain represents a powerful means of learning because it deals with attitudes, values, feelings, and interests. Affective learning is a continuous process that goes beyond the typical classroom environment. Role-playing, group discussion, and brainstorming are some of the teaching techniques noted in this book that represent excellent ways to get participants to deal with safety issues, attitudes toward change, and so on. After individuals are made aware of an issue (receiving), the next higher level is to get them to attend or react to it (responding). They then need to value it. For example, an employee will recognize the worth of other coworkers by giving assistance without being asked, working cooperatively with them, using tact in replying to coworkers, and sharing ideas freely with them. Hohn (1995) noted that attitudes and values that were initially external to an individual have yet to be learned to the point of becoming part of a person's habit pattern. He noted that in

> information-processing terms, learning in the early stages of the taxonomy is not yet based on an interconnected network of schemas. As additional experience is integrated into cognitive structure, however, affective learning at the later stages of the taxonomy is considered to be internal, or part of the individual's

habitual way of perceiving and responding to the environment (pp. 301-302).

It should be noted that affective learning does not occur independently nor is it taught in isolation from the cognitive learning.

Teaching in the affective domain using the Web involves approaching attitudes first through the cognitive domain—appealing first to reason through understanding and analyzing pertinent information. For example, if the objective is to teach acceptance of people of other racial or ethnic groups, positive attitudes can be fostered through **synchronous** dialogue on the issue, using presentations and interviews, as well as through **asynchronous** activities, which involve learners in learning more about other cultures.

Keefe (1987) has examined affective learning styles and stated that learners vary along a continuum in such matters as the levels of anxiety they can feel comfortable with and their tolerances for frustration. Also, learners vary in their preferences for learning through interaction with others or working alone. MacKeracher (1997), drawing upon the ideas of Keefe and others, has noted that facilitators tend to plan initial activities according to their own preferred styles and that it is important to use a variety of approaches to assist all learners in optimizing their learning potential.

Web-based learning is not well suited for developing kinesthetic skills because there is little opportunity for modeling or for feedback to accompany practice. Nevertheless, the rudiments of some psychomotor skills are taught on some physical fitness sites. These sites use graphics and text to explain exercises and to alert learners to signs they may recognize of appropriate or poor performance. Videos presented on the Web also are used to model correct performance of physical exercises. However, the impossibility of feedback on learners' performance remains a drawback at this time to teaching kinesthetic skills through Web-based means.

The *psychomotor domain* consists of five major categories—imitation, manipulation, precision, articulation, and naturalization (Armstrong, 1970). **Kinesthetic,** or psychomotor domain, learning involves movement that is required or that in some way facilitates the learning process. Development of sports skills is an obvious area in which physical movement plays a major role in learning. Movement and manipulation of equipment and materials are several of the 13 strategies discussed in this book. Demonstration, when the session calls for participants to replicate the presentation, is an activity that utilizes the kinesthetic domain. MacKeracher (1997) noted five phases in psychomotor learning: (a) modeling, in which the facilitator demonstrates the skill; (b) approximating, in which learners try out the required motions; (c) fading, in which each learner tries the skill alone "in a safe but realistic environment" (p. 160); (d) soloing, further practice in which the learner is self-directed; and (e) discussing the skill learning, in which facilitator and learner(s) reflect on the skill and discuss adaptations (pp. 160-161).

Practically speaking, any activity that involves tactile learning probably also calls for kinesthetic activity. Such activities as developing computer skills and practicing safety procedures obviously require kinesthetic learning. However, numerous other applications are possible. Lazear (1991) makes use of kinesthetic learning to teach vocabulary. This is accomplished by introducing the words (unfamiliar to the participants) and providing physical movements (without words) as the definition. Participants observe and then practice the motions associated with the vocabulary words. Afterwards, participants are shown a group of definitions and find, perhaps to their surprise, that they are able to associate the verbal definitions with the appropriate vocabulary words. Creative classroom practitioners find opportunities to include this domain for variety and effectiveness in the teaching-learning process.

Environment and Effective Learning

Teaching ordinarily occurs when the teacher interacts with one or more learners. However, feelings, emotions, or attitudes may block learning. Online practitioners cannot begin to dispel all of these blocks, but they must address some of them, especially boredom, confusion, irritability, and fear among the participants.

How the online instruction is set up can either facilitate or impede the learning process. Use of online software and other factors influence the attitudes of both presenter and learners. The presentation of the online materials sets the tone. As much as possible, the trainer or instructor must monitor the appropriateness of how the content is being received in an attempt to ensure that the process of learning online is helpful rather than detrimental. Assessment of the online materials must be ongoing throughout the session.

In addition, it is important to recognize the importance of the trainer's mental attitude as an environmental factor. Individuals who approach their responsibilities with enthusiasm for the subject, confidence in their abilities, and appropriate preparation for the session will be well on their way to avoiding blocks to learning. If the teacher also demonstrates genuine acceptance of each of the participants, this quality—together with adequate preparation—should help avoid or eliminate the learning deterrents that can be managed and controlled by the classroom practitioner.

Effective Teaching Skills

That which is seen as effective teaching or presenting by one observer may be considered poor by another. This phenomenon occurs because each person's values and experiences are different from everyone else's. However, although it may be difficult to come to agreement about what good presenting or teaching is, effective teaching can be demonstrated. The effective online practitioner is an individual who is able to bring about intended outcomes in a consistent manner.

Although the nature of learning is itself important, different online practitioners may seek and achieve favorable outcomes using different techniques. All of these online practitioners would be judged effective. This leads us to the prime criterion for assessment of effective teaching or training—a positive correlation between intent and outcome. Thus, if we exclude intent, participants' achievements would be random or accidental, and if participants at presentations do not achieve the intended outcomes, the trainer or teacher cannot be considered effective.

Smith (1969) noted that a teacher who is well trained is prepared in four major areas. First, this teacher has command of the theoretical knowledge of human behavior and learning. This includes motivation and reinforcement techniques. Second, the teacher displays a positive attitude toward the subject matter and the participants, in order to foster learning and development. Third, the teacher possesses command of the subject area that she or he will be presenting. This subject knowledge includes not only presentation methods but the implementation, evaluation, and feedback phases as well. Finally, the well-trained teacher employs technical strategies that result in meaningful learning experiences, such as those outlined in this book.

Online practitioners must be able to make solid decisions concerning (a) content selection, (b) appropriate involvement by participants, (c) demonstration that appropriate learning has occurred, and (d) the presenter's role as facilitator of learning. Effective trainers and teachers must plan, implement, and evaluate themselves as well as their participants in order to hone their skills.

Planning is perhaps the most important strategy for assuring better online teaching. As the old saying goes, "It wasn't raining when Noah built the ark." Noah planned ahead; so must teachers and other presenters. Essential aspects of planning include determining the learning objectives, content, and teaching techniques and deciding what participants must do in order to demonstrate that learning has occurred. One also must consider the anticipatory set, wherein the trainer gains the attention and interest of learners, and the closure, during which the online practitioner brings the session to an appropriate conclusion.

Qualities of Effective Trainers and Educators

Successful educators have in common several key characteristics. These may be categorized under traits of character and personality, interpersonal skills, expectations of self and students, possession of an adequate knowledge base, instructional skills and methods, and classroom management skills. Numerous surveys have found that the most effective educators are perceived as caring, enthusiastic, consistent, and impartial in their dealings with students.

The adage "They won't care what you know 'til they know that you care" fits here. If participants believe the online practitioner cares about them and about their learning, they also will attribute other important character and personality traits to the classroom practitioner—such as being patient and sensitive to their needs and having a sense of purpose. When demonstrated, these qualities in the trainer help students have a positive disposition toward learning and meet the classroom practitioner's expectations.

Excellent online practitioners expect their participants to have high standards of behavior and academic achievement. These classroom practitioners expect participants to provide appropriate feedback and to be involved in their own learning, as opposed to being passive in class. Trainers and teachers expect students to be prepared for learning sessions and to follow through with review and practice on their own, to further enhance their growth.

Master trainers and educators likewise have high expectations of themselves. They see themselves as self-reliant directors and facilitators of learning and as role models. They have well-defined personal goals. They are rigorous in self-appraisal and work consistently toward even greater personal development.

Proficient educators possess excellent communication skills, get along well with others, are capable leaders, and are able to persuade participants to extend themselves beyond former boundaries. They readily establish rapport with students and other professionals. They learn participants' e-mail names as quickly as possible and make a practice of addressing students by their preferred e-mail nicknames. Their caring attitude is felt in their appreciation of the unique characteristics of each student and in their encouragement of participants to expect the best of themselves. In addition, master trainers and educators are able to bring a sense of humor to the task. They are ethical, respectful of others, and appropriately assertive as they engage students in the learning process.

Obviously, excellent online presenters must possess a mastery of their particular discipline. They usually exhibit special talents in their area of expertise. They continue to update themselves in their content areas and develop new skills and strategies of instruction. Expert teachers recognize the importance of appropriate pacing so that difficult concepts are dealt with more slowly and review is fast paced. Online teachers make every attempt to give directions clearly and in logical sequence. Competent educators make frequent checks for understanding and provide for individual learning differences despite environmental variables. They encourage students and participants in their workshops to go beyond the elementary learning of information and be able to apply their knowledge and practice the higher order thinking skills of analysis, synthesis, and evaluation. They encourage participants' questions. They also refer students to other sources, rather than have them rely solely on a single textbook.

Finally, proficient educators, whether in the classroom or in other settings, find appropriate ways to support participants in their efforts to gain insights, and they always attempt to reward improvement and success. They incorporate diverse teaching strategies and use effective mediavisuals to enhance learning. They respect participants' points of view, create readiness to learn by helping participants see how the material will be useful to them, and assist students in transferring new learning. They illustrate abstract concepts with real-life examples.

To accomplish all this, trainers and teachers must possess much energy and enthusiasm. Typically this is done via compressed video segments of the instructor that are embedded within the content of online materials. Instructors need to be expressive, making use of eye contact, moving appropriately toward their students, and gesturing appropriately as they communicate. Energy is evident long before students and instructor meet because effective educators invest themselves in planning and developing a variety of instructional strategies, such as those presented in this book. They avoid merely trying to "wing it."

Effective presenters who do compressed video are careful to

avoid meaningless motions of their hands, which might distract or confuse students at the receiving end of the online instruction. They keep their hands out of their pockets, avoid leaning on the podium except as a point of emphasis or intensity, and avoid disruptive pacing back and forth. They do gesture and move about the room, but with purpose rather than as evidence of nervousness.

Skills for Web Instructors

Web instructors do far more than connect learners with vast sources of information. According to Driscoll (1998) and Beer (2000), they also facilitate meaningful **synchronous** and **asynchronous** interaction with the information and with other learners. Instructing in the virtual classroom involves a new approach and special attention even to your former instructional approaches.

1. *Choose your words carefully.* Cues such as vocal tone and body language will not be as available online. Also, be sparing in your use of ALL CAPITALS, which could be interpreted as shouting.

2. *Keep Web lectures short.* Intersperse lecture segments with opportunities for learner participation. Allow them to contribute their knowledge and experience. Moderate **synchronous** discussions or invite **asynchronous** contributions to an electronic message board. Ask questions of individual learners, and call on others to answer. Acknowledge learners' contributions. Grade learners on the quality of their contributions as well as on their tests and projects.

3. *Assign work that requires collaboration.* Encourage learners to contact experts or other students for information and ideas. Divide the class into small groups and have them develop group projects or class presentations.

4. *Schedule online office hours.* Be consistent about keeping posted times. Consider them as opportunities for **synchronous** exchanges—times when you can respond to learners' ideas and needs as you would during office appointments.

5. *Encourage e-mail messaging.* This will provide learners with **asynchronous** opportunities to reach you. Consider

encouraging learners to exchange e-mail addresses with one another as another option for **asynchronous** collaboration.

6. *Provide a syllabus.* Post on the Website a schedule of lectures, lessons, assignments, and due dates. Also include your grading criteria and grading scale. Post any instructor's information (office address and hours, telephone number, e-mail address) you wish learners to have.

7. *Provide a journal of class activities.* This will supplement and reinforce the information contained in the syllabus. Be careful to keep the journal current.

8. *Summarize and review periodically.* This will allow for clarification and reinforcement of ideas. **Synchronous** summary and review times also provide excellent opportunities to respond to students' questions.

9. *Keep the class size to between 10 and 20 learners.* You need enough participants for collaboration, but not so many that you are overwhelmed with posting, responding, and evaluating. Managing class size also helps learners by keeping **synchronous** discussions within reasonable limits.

Thoughts for Trainers About the Characteristics of Adult Learners

Adults enter the learning environment prepared for and expecting to be active participants. Therefore, instructors and trainers of adult learners should plan with these characteristics in mind:

✗ Adults bring relevant, real-life experience to the classroom.

✗ Adults expect learning to be meaningful within the context of their ordinary lives.

✗ Adults naturally adapt and apply their learning beyond the classroom.

✗ Adults enjoy analysis, synthesis, and problem-solving activities.

✗ Adults adapt well to interactive, problem-centered opportunities.

✗ Adults want to plan some of their projects and other learning activities.

✗ Adults vary in their preferred learning styles.

Keeping these qualities in mind, trainers and facilitators must plan activities that make use of learners' prior knowledge and experience, develop interactive learning experiences, use a variety of approaches for teaching the same concepts, and adapt to the needs and expectations of each group. This makes it imperative that those planning and implementing classes, workshops, and technology-based delivery know their participants' needs and experiences ahead of time.

Purpose of the Training

Trainers may or may not be involved in a needs analysis to determine the reasons for the training. In either case, it is essential to determine several things beforehand, especially (a) what need is to be met; (b) who the participants will be, (c) what participants' prior experiences are with regard, to the topic; (d) the relationships (formal and informal) of the participants to one another, (e) what the expected outcomes are, (f) how the training will be reinforced once workers return to their jobs, and (g) what kind of evaluation will be conducted and when the evaluation(s) will occur.

Evaluation of the Training

Most training sessions or modules end with some type of learner evaluation. According to Kirkpatrick (1994), however, the Level I type so often conducted merely assesses trainees' immediate reactions and does little or nothing to inform trainers or their employers about the long-term effectiveness of the training. For the evaluation to be helpful, four levels are recommended: (a) Level I—a simple check sheet to assess learners attitudes at the end of the training, (b) Level II—a brief check of learners' knowledge and skills at the end of training (often this takes the form of pre/post tests to compare what learners knew before with what they learned during the training), (c) Level III—conducted in the job setting shortly after workers return to measure improved performance, and (d) Level

IV—conducted several weeks or months after the training to assess long-term effects of the training (Kirkpatrick, 1994).

If training is to be effective long-term, supervisors must be involved in the planning phase to determine the objectives and expected outcomes of the training. It is also essential that supervisors and upper-level managers be in agreement, especially regarding areas in which trainers are to facilitate change in attitudes, safety practices, and so forth. Without managerial support, such training is bound to be ineffectual.

Web-Based Learning

Most educational institutions at every level as well as large businesses and industries incorporate a variety of technology-based educational opportunities. Computer modules and packaged video programs, for example, have been in use for a number of years for asynchronous learning beyond the classroom and for just-in-time instruction for workers. Web-based instruction encompasses all the advantages of former technology plus several others.

The possibility for asynchronous learning (those learning experiences that do not require instructors and learners to participate together at the same time) has been obvious from the initiation of technology-based activities. As noted in Driscoll (1998) and Beer (2000) books, a new concept with weblearning is that activities may be planned for either asynchronous or synchronous participation (both instructor and learner(s) participate at the same time, although usually not at the same location). Synchronous learning activities provide for real-time interaction among participants who are at different geographical locations. Thus, the needs and expectations of adults with other real-life demands can be met—including needs for interaction—without many of the constraints imposed by travel and scheduling barriers.

> ✗ Satellite instruction involves students and trainers participating **synchronously** via TV beamed to prearranged satellite locations. This method may involve presentations plus (a) telephoning in questions and comments to be shared by the presenter(s), (b) active learner participation

through monitors that transmit to the various locations, and/ or (c) planned group activities at each location following the presentation. (Satellite instruction can also be videotaped for **asynchronous** use in other learning situations.)

✗ Online courses and workshops are frequently established through special Web pages just for that specific audience. Through this option, educators design a Web page to link students with course materials (including video) and to supplemental sites on the World Wide Web to increase learner interaction with a variety of other information sources. Listservs, including response options similar to chat rooms, offer further options for **synchronous or asynchronous** interactive learning through online courses.

✗ Traditional classes can also incorporate Web-based instruction, and this often provides at least three major advantages. First, it brings additional knowledge sources into the classroom. Second, when several options are presented simultaneously, it encourages lively exploration in a learner-directed environment. Finally, this **synchronous** option provides an excellent learning situation for developing learners' computer skills. Especially when neophytes are paired with more experienced learners, classroom Internet use provides a safe learning environment for computer literacy training as well as for the other instructional objectives of the course.

Table 1.1 shows a variety of possible Web applications of the Web activities classified according to Bloom's taxonomy. These activities can be adapted to classroom use or to Web-based courses. They provide for both **synchronous and asynchronous** participation.

A Word About How to Use the Planning and Evaluation Sheets

To assist the classroom practitioner in using the techniques included in this book, we have developed and placed at the end of each chapter planning and evaluation sheets for each respective technique. Planning is an essential aspect of online instruction. The planning worksheet will assist classroom practitioners in thinking

Table 1.1
An Example of Web Learning
According to Bloom's Taxonomy

Level of Learning	Specification of Learning Activity	Examples of Web-Learning Activities
Knowledge, Understanding, and Analysis	Identify the scope of their organization's needs and opportunities. *[independent learning]*	Search the Web for information on your organization's area of expertise. Identify and describe the needs and opportunities of the industry. If possible, join a customer service chat room and analyze customer issues and needs.
Analysis, Synthesis, and Evaluation	Develop ideas and approaches to answering needs. *[independent and interactive learning]*	Access a Web site for an organization similar to yours. Analyze and evaluate its product or service efforts to solve a particular problem that your organization is facing. Moderate an asynchronous discussion about the problem.
Synthesis, Application, and Evaluation	Apply ideas to meet application requirements. *[independent or interactive learning]*	Create a plan to address the problem you identified and publish your plan. Ask experts to analyze and comment, using an HTML editor so readers can see who made which comments.
Application	Document and disseminate ideas using groupware, trainers, and apprentices. *[interactive learning]*	Document the strategy that you used to investigate the problem and publish your strategy. Create an asynchronous Web discussion so others can study your methodology and discuss it with you.

through and preparing for the technique they plan to use. It will be a helpful reference to the concepts and objectives of the session and a reminder of materials and equipment needs. Finally, this page may serve as the session outline.

The evaluation sheet will help educators who are concerned about their own professional development assess their effectiveness after each training session. Another valuable source of feedback is from the individual learners. Each prospective trainer and trainee can offer valuable insights for improving the teaching and learning process. It is recommended, therefore, that the lecturer use this sheet for self-evaluation and that he or she also request similar feedback from the audience to validate self-perceptions and reveal any discrepancies.

A Word About How to Use the Checklist

The selection of a teaching technique involves consideration of the learners (number, background, experience), the desired cognitive outcomes, and appropriate sensory involvement. Use of the Table 1.2 checklist on page 25 will facilitate the classroom practitioner's task of choosing the best technique for a given situation. Each instructional method presented in this volume (listed at the top of the checklist) has been marked according to the appropriate cognitive levels (as identified in Bloom's taxonomy) and according to the type(s) of sensory involvement that would be (or could be) helpful in using that technique (Brewer, 1997).

An excellent step-by-step method for using this book would be to (a) consider the learning needs and desired outcomes for a training session, (b) use this checklist to select one or two appropriate techniques, (c) turn to the chapter(s) treating the preferred strategies, (d) read the chapters, and (e) make a final selection.

Conclusion

This book is presented with several purposes in mind: (a) to help individuals become better educators, (b) to serve as an ongoing reference for teaching fundamentals, and (c) to challenge experienced teachers to expand their repertoire of skills in working with their various audiences. Veterans of the profession may find new teaching methods in this book. Teachers and trainers who are just beginning will find a ready source that contains a wide variety of teaching techniques. Instructions are detailed enough for novices to select and implement them, using the planning sheets at the end of each chapter. Evaluation sheets on the pages following the planning sheets should be used for further growth and development.

This volume contains methods for working with a wide range of learners—from individual instruction offered to persons encountering the material for the first time to audiences for whom the learning session is an enrichment experience. It includes techniques that lead students and trainees to develop new skills and methods for presenting to larger groups an abundance of information in a logical, interesting fashion. We trust and hope that this book will be useful to all educators seeking to improve their teaching techniques.

References

Armstrong, R. J. (1970). *Developing and writing behavioral objectives.* Tucson, AZ: Educational Innovators Press.

Beer, V. (2000). *The Web learning fieldbook: Using the World Wide Web to build workplace learning environments.* San Francisco: Jossey-Bass/Pfeiffer.

Bloom, B. S. (1976). *Human characteristics and school learning.* New York, NY: McGraw-Hill.

Bloom, B. S., Englehart, M. B., Furst, E. J., Hill, W. H., & Krathwohl, D. R. (1956). *Taxonomy of educational objectives: The classification of educational goals. Handbook I: Cognitive domain.* New York: Longman Green.

Brewer, E. W. (1997). *13 proven ways to get your message across: The essential reference for teachers, trainers, prsenters, and speakers.* Thousand Oaks, CA: Corwin.

Driscoll, M. (1998). *Web-based training: Using technology to design adult learning experiences.* San Francisco: Jossey-Bass/Pfeiffer.

Henson, K. T. (1996). *Methods and strategies for teaching in secondary and middle schools* (3rd ed.). New York: Longman.

Hohn, R. L. (1995). *Classroom learning and teaching.* New York: Longman.

Hunter, M. (1990). *Mastery teaching.* El Segundo, CA: TIP.

Keefe, J. W. (1987). *Learning style theory and practice.* Reston, VA: National Association of Secondary School Principals.

Kirkpatrick, D. L. (1994). *Evaluating training programs: The four levels.* San Francisco: Berrett-Koehler.

Krathwohl, D. R., Bloom, B. S., & Masia, B. B. (1964). *Taxonomy of educational objectives. Handbook II: Affective domain.* New York: David McKay.

Lazear, D. (1991). *Seven ways of knowing: Teaching for multiple intelligences.* Palatine, IL: Skylight.

MacKeracher, D. (1997). *Making sense of adult learning.* Toronto, Canada: Culture Concepts.

Malone, J. C. (1991). *Theories of learning: A historical approach.* Belmont, CA: Wadsworth.

Mazur, J. E. (1990). *Learning and behavior* (2nd ed.). Englewood Cliffs, NJ: Prentice Hall.

Miller, A. (1991). *Personality types: A modern synthesis.* Calgary, Canada: University of Calgary Press.

Simpson, E. J. (1972). *The classification of educational objectives in the psychomotor domain. The psychomotor domain* (Vol. 3). Washington, DC: Gryphon House.

Smith, B. O. (1969). *Teachers for the real world.* Washington, DC: American Association of Colleges for Teacher Education.

Thorndike, E. L. (1905). *The elements of psychology.* New York: Seiler.

Table 1.2
Checklist According to Cognitive
Outcomes and Sensory Involvement

	Instructional Technique												
	Lecture	Small-Group Discussion	Role-Playing	Case Study	Demonstration	Panel	Inquiry Method	Buzz Groups	Programmed Instruction	Directed Study	Experiment	Brainstorming	Questioning
Cognitive Levels													
Information	✓	✓	✓	✓	✓	✓	✓		✓	✓	✓	✓	✓
Comprehension	✓	✓	✓	✓	✓	✓	✓		✓	✓	✓	✓	✓
Application			✓	✓	✓	✓	✓	✓	✓	✓	✓	✓	✓
Analysis		✓	✓	✓	✓	✓	✓	✓	✓	✓	✓	✓	✓
Synthesis	✓		✓	✓	✓	✓	✓	✓	✓	✓	✓	✓	✓
Evaluation	✓	✓	✓	✓	✓	✓	✓	✓	✓	✓	✓	✓	✓
Sensory Appeal													
Auditory (sound)	✓	✓	✓	✓	✓	✓	✓	✓	✓	✓	✓	✓	✓
Visual (sight)	✓	✓	✓	✓	✓	✓	✓	✓	✓	✓	✓	✓	✓
Tactile (touch)			✓		✓		✓			✓	✓		
Olfactory (smell)					✓						✓		
Gustatory (taste)					✓						✓		
Instructional Methods When You Want to. . .													
Only Give Information	✓						✓						
Encourage Participation		✓	✓	✓	✓	✓	✓	✓	✓	✓	✓	✓	✓
Provide Hands-on Experience					✓				✓		✓		
Get Participants to Respond		✓	✓	✓	✓	✓	✓	✓				✓	✓
Have Participants Simulate Interpersonal Communications		✓	✓	✓	✓		✓	✓				✓	✓
Give Problem-Solving Opportunities to Participants		✓	✓	✓	✓		✓	✓				✓	✓
Instructional Method According to Teaching and Learning													
Teaching Method	✓				✓	✓			✓				
Teaching Method to Aid Learning									✓			✓	✓
Learning Method			✓	✓			✓				✓	✓	
Teaching-Learning Method	✓				✓								

CHAPTER 2

ONLINE LEARNING:
A HISTORICAL PERSPECTIVE

T hink of teaching and you probably visualize a traditional classroom. A subject matter "master" is standing before a group of students
anticipating something new. Today, not only have the student and
teacher changed, but also the classroom itself has evolved beyond
the classroom walls to the world. The use of the Internet has facilitated this change.

How did we get to the present state of online learning? Can
we learn from the historic progression that has brought us to this
point? Can you extend your teaching beyond the classroom without
abandoning the teaching skills you have acquired in the traditional
setting? You can do just that by understanding the past and continu-
ing progression of online teaching and learning. You can pick up at
any stage of its development and add to your teaching repertoire and
experiences for your students.

Early Years

The very earliest form of an extended classroom, or distance education, was paper-based correspondence. As early as 1840, Issac Pittman was teaching shorthand in England by correspondence (Curzon, 1977). This form of distance education was just the beginning of what we are experiencing today. It was thought of as an educational experience that, at least part of the time, had the instructor and students at a distance from each other.

As far back as 1928, a Columbia University doctoral dissertation found no differences in test scores of college classroom and correspondence study students enrolled in the same subjects (Crump, 1928). As technology changed, so did the methods of transferring information. Video, radio, and television were added to the mechanisms used for information transfer. All the time, the transfer was basically from the teacher to students, with students providing feedback in the form of mailed-in assignments to the teacher. This form of distance education, as noted in Figure 2.1, can be best described as a period of autonomy and independence. When the independence of the learner is valued and acquisition of knowledge is successful, this form of distance education has achieved the desired goal for learning.

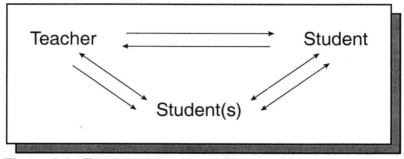

Figure 2.1. Teacher and student autonomy and independence.

Independent learning was taking place through television and teleconferencing. By the 1980s research found

1. There is no evidence to support the idea that face-to-face instruction is the optimum delivery method.

2. Instruction by teleconferencing can facilitate learning **as well** or better than classroom instruction.

3. The absence of face-to-face contact is **not detrimental** to the learning process. (Weingand, 1984)

Creation of the traditional classroom setting through the available media was achieved. The expectation here was student independence derived from successful completion and mastery of the subject matter presented.

Recent Years

Establishing an Online Presence

The first attempts of instructors to incorporate computer experiences into the traditional classroom are usually in terms of adding enrichment to the classroom lecture. Educational sites that foster the learning experience beyond what the instructor has prepared can be shown in the classroom or used as assignments for further study.

The availability of computers, software programs, and Internet connections often dictate the way this material can be used. When computers are scarce, a virtual trip to a computer destination becomes almost like bringing a guest lecturer to class. If computers are available to individual students in a laboratory, the lab can be used to reinforce or apply the content of a lecture. Once this has been successfully accomplished, the instructor usually finds opportunities to let the students explore information on the topics related to the area of study, and new resources quickly become available to all.

As students become more involved in the use of computers and instructors become more comfortable with the technology, the next step is often putting the course syllabus online. This enables students to have access anytime and provides a mechanism for sharing with prospective students the overview of the course. Reference lists and URL sites for additional resource material or exercises may also accompany the syllabus. Many times, the addition of class notes to the site is done to assist the students in getting the most out of the material. It helps students have access to material at times other than regular class time, and it gives instructors an organized format to answer routine questions from students who may have missed class or who need to check on course requirements or assignments. All of this is still supplemental to regular classroom experiences.

Online Lectures

Taking the first big step toward putting a class online means turning the first lecture into online experience. Here the instructor puts into online format the material that would be given to students in the classroom. First attempts are usually detailed outlines, Power-Point™ slides, or simple HTML pages. They may be interjected with visuals, direct quotes, and side trips to additional online sites. As the instructor's technology skills develop, he or she may include audio or video streaming segments to emphasize the material. All of this is still using the traditional model of a classroom-learning situation that emphasizes the imparting of information to students. It can increase the goal of student independence because of the responsibility placed upon the student to take action to receive the material, rather than sitting in a passive classroom.

Has this method been successful? The Carnegie Foundation, in considering a possible restructuring of a university of technological change, reviewed many comparative studies of traditional and online courses. As has been typical of sound research findings, the reseacher (Bates, 1997) stated that there were no significant differences in student-learning outcomes for courses taught in traditional classrooms compared to online courses.

There have been dramatic changes in delivery methods for training programs. The American Society for Training and Development (ASTD) projections from 1996 to the year 2000 stated that the percentage of training time delivery by instructor-led methods will decrease from 80% to 55%. At the same time, learning technology methods are expected to increase from 10% to 35% (Piskurich &

Sanders, 1998). The Internet has changed the way we do business, education and training are part of the change. "Using the Web, training and development professionals can leverage instructional resources in ways never before possible" (Ellis, Wagner, & Longmire, 1999, p. xiii).

By the late 1990s, resources had become available for instructors to go beyond the goal of independence of the learner in online experiences. **Learning interdependence** could be sustained by collaborative experiences between teachers and learners and/or among learners with other learners. Management systems for online courses now allow various types of interactions and provide means for tracking involvement. These techniques for interaction and sharing make the communication pattern more complex. These patterns include both synchronous (real time) and asynchronous (delayed) communication. Figure 2.2 identifies several techniques for interaction.

Discussion boards
Small-group formation
Chat availability for class and small groups
E-mailing the entire class or selected class members
Group or individual assignment posting

Figure 2.2. Techniques for interaction.

As increased involvement and interaction occurs, learning begins to transcend acquisition of knowledge and skills to comprehension, application, analysis, and even synthesis. Students are not just accepting information but are dealing with it in discussion or application form. They become involved beyond listening and taking in facts. They question and engage in problem solving in their interactions with the teacher and other students. The teacher role evolves beyond content "master" and presenter to facilitator of learning experiences. The teacher directs the learning experience and observes as students take charge of their own learning. This is illustrated in Figure 2.3.

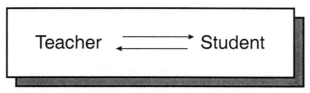

Figure 2.3. Teacher/student and student/
teacher interaction.

In the 1999 *Journal of Computing in Higher Education,* Navarro and Shoemaker reported that cyber learning can be as effective as traditional classroom learning. In the study, they reported the two groups achieved at approximately the same level as measured by test scores. The findings of this study appear to provide preliminary evidence that cyber learning can be as effective as learning in the traditional classroom (Navarro & Shoemaker, 1999).

It must be noted that for successful learning experiences to occur, someone must first identify the level or type of learning to take place. Learning can be successful when the expectations are independence of the learner and mastery of information. Learning experiences can be straight lecture in a large lecture hall or in an online lecture presentation involving words, and audio and visual effects. However, if the learning expected is required to go beyond the beginning stage of knowledge acquisition, the experiences must involve the learner and must allow for opportunities to interact with the information and with others including other learners and the teacher. If the latter is the goal, the experiences created by the teacher-facilitator are possible in a traditional classroom setting or in an online form of instruction. It is not the place that becomes important but how to best use the techniques for learning. This book will help you put to use skills for facilitating learning, traditionally used in the classroom, and now possible in a cyber environment.

Future Years

Is there a next step in this development that we can see coming even now? We are learning more through research about the online learning experience every day. For this experience to be successful, we must understand the special needs of learners in the online environment. The technology at first is a novelty to some and a barrier to others. As teachers and facilitators of learning, we must prepare learners to go beyond the technology. It has been said that the technology must become transparent for the learner to begin the interaction with content. Studies are now being conducted that will help us to understand online learners and how interaction with the technology may affect learning experiences. Once we know more about the barriers to learning, the motivation for learning, and the progression to successful learning online, we will be able to provide better experiences to ensure success.

Multidimensional Learning Experiences

One could believe that the next phase of online learning would be even more learner driven. The learner who selects the experiences from materials prepared and organized by instructors would manage online experiences. Learners would have branching learning opportunities to take them into different paths, depending on their knowledge and personal educational goals. Development of such materials is now possible. However, the technical skill needed to develop them is beyond most classroom instructors' or trainers' computer skills. In the future, however, just as classroom management tools have made putting a class online possible, user-friendly products for developing complex learning experiences will be accessible to all. The multidimensional learning experiences are displayed in Figure 2.4.

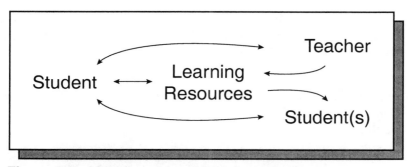

Figure 2.4. Multidimensional learning experiences.

The availability of higher definition computers and the improved preparation and transfer of video and audio will make attempts at streaming video today seem archaic. The ease of synchronous communication (both audio and visual) will bring students into sight and facilitators into students' homes virtually face-to-face. The next generation of online learning will go far beyond our imagination or technical ability.

Conclusion

The incentive for online learning may at first be convenience for the student. However, when the computer is used to move beyond traditional classroom walls, opportunities for learning expand. Education is becoming an experience of learning and sharing for students and teachers as we move to a community of learners online. The sharing can go beyond the teacher-student alliance to provide significant opportunity for virtual alliances with organizations and industries that contribute to the learning experience.

We can only begin to predict the changes in store for us. Our skills and abilities to transform the cyber classroom into the leaning center of the future will depend upon our ability to provide a variety of experiences for the learner and our desire to continue learning ourselves. Parts 2, 3, and 4 of this book will show you how you can begin by using many traditional classroom techniques in a new way for these online experiences.

References

Bates, A. W. (1997, June). *Restructuring the university for technological change.* Paper presented at the Carnegie Foundation for the Advancement of Teaching Conference: What Kind of University? London.

Crump, R. E. (1928). *Correspondence and class extension work in Oklahoma.* Unpublished doctoral dissertation, Teachers College, Columbia University.

Curzon, A. J. (1977). Correspondence education in England and in the Netherlands. *Comparative Education, 13*(3), 249-261.

Ellis, A. L., Wagner, E. D., & Longmire, W. R. (1999). *Managing web-based training.* Alexandria, VA: American Society for Training and Development.

Navarro, P., & Shoemaker, J. (1999). The power of cyber learning: An empirical test. *Journal of Computing in Higher Education, 11*(1), 13-15.

Piskurich, G. M., & Sanders, E. S. (1998). *ASTD models for learning technologies.* Alexandria, VA: American Society for Training and Development.

Spooner, F., Jordan, L., Algozzine, B., & Spooner, M. (1999). Student ratings of instruction in distance learning and on-campus classes. *The Journal of Educational Research, 92*(3), 132-140.

VanderMeer, A. W. (1950). *Relative effectiveness of instruction by films exclusively, films plus study guides, and standard lecture methods* (Technical Report No. SDC 269-7-130). Port Washington, NY: U. S. Navy Training Devices Center.

Weingand, D. E. (1984). *Telecommunications and the traditional classroom: A study of the delivery of education.* Madison: University of Wisconsin.

CHAPTER 3

MOVING FROM TRADITIONAL CLASSROOM INSTRUCTION TO ONLINE INSTRUCTION

With opportunities to learn *anywhere* and *anytime* becoming more plentiful and alternative instructional delivery methods and systems becoming more commonplace, record numbers of teachers and trainers offer, or are preparing to offer, online instruction.

The term *online instruction* may be operationally defined in a variety of ways. As suggested in Chapters 1 and 2, online instruction represents *instructional text-based* and *multimedia-based presentation formats used in a web-based delivery system.* This generic definition emanates from public and private sector research about and practical applications of learning technologies. Online instruction represents a broad spectrum of instructional possibilities—ranging from posting course information on the World Wide Web, to augmenting instruction with web-based resources, and to teaching fully web-based courses and programs in which instructors and learners never meet face-to-face.

The Emerging Role
of Learning Technologies

In the American Society for Training & Development (ASTD) *State of the Industry Report*, McMurrer, Van Buren, and Woodwell (2000) reported that, based upon 1998-1999 data, the average firm in the ASTD Benchmarking Service delivered 8.5 % of its training and development using learning technologies. Future corporate projections suggest the spread of learning technologies is likely to continue. Likewise, use of learning technologies in public education has grown to such an extent that in the United States each state now employs a state-level educational technology coordinator to facilitate instructional technology application and integration in public schools.

For several years, ASTD has grouped the types of learning technologies into two categories. Category 1 includes learning technologies used as *formats for presenting training* such as text-only computer-based training (CBT) and multimedia. Category 2 consists of learning technologies used as *methods or systems for distributing training*, examples of which include company intranets, cable TV, and CD-ROMs. For the purpose of discussion in this text, online instruction represents *both categories*—formats for presenting and methods or systems for distributing instruction.

According to Piskurich and Sanders (1998), the two ASTD categories for grouping learning technologies support a third category, namely, *methods of instruction* such as lecture and demonstration. These methods are detailed in the subsequent chapters of this text.

Piskurich and Sanders (1998) reported that although additional research is needed concerning learning retention rates using learning technologies, these are cheaper and more accessible as instructional formats and methods than traditional classroom instruction.

Piskurich (1998), in describing future learning technology forces, projects that online instruction will continue to develop and become a standard for technology-based training as problems with bandwidth and speed are solved. But McMurrer et al. (2000) indicate that despite probable growth in companies using learning technologies, data imply that organizations are finding technology-based training difficult to master. Implementation challenges include not only technological barriers but also pressure to demonstrate return on investment in a new way of learning.

Ideally, technology plays a transparent supporting role in the learning process. As shown in the top graphic within Figure 3.1, appropriate integration of learning technologies casts technology in the background. The technology supports development of instructional relationships. As depicted in the bottom graphic within Figure 3.1, gratuitous and/or awkwardly or inappropriately employed learning technologies can actually juxtapose the role and importance of technology allowing it to compete with the learning process. Left unchecked, such competition diverts instructors' and learners' attention.

Instructional Relationship Building in Online Instruction

As instructors consider adapting to online instruction, careful reflection is needed concerning the critical, integrated process of instructional relationship building thought possible and likely with traditional instruction. How does facilitation of this process translate to and occur in a cyber-learning environment? Table 3.1 shows the importance of relationship building between instructor and learner, learner and content, and learner with learner collaboration associated with effective instruction. Although neither completely hierarchical nor sequential, frequently these relationships grow in linear order. Cultivation of a relationship between the instructor and the learner subsequently *supports* cultivation of a relationship between the learner and the content, which, in turn, *equips* the learner to participate in meaningful collaboration with other learners for the purposes of content-related problem solving and decision making.

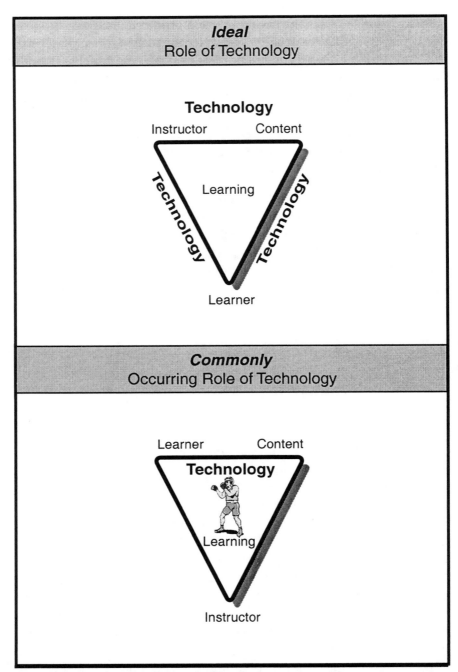

Figure 3.1. Technology's role in the learning process.

Table 3.1
Tri-Focal Instructional Relationship Building

Relationship	Lens Focus	Line of Vision or Perspective Served
Instructor and Learner	Preliminary and Foundational[a]	Initial and intermittent clarity of instructional scope, purpose, and sequence; learner performance expectations; and learning achievement
		Navigation facilitation through the instructional experience to enhance learning processes and achievement
Learner and Content	Primary and Peripheral	Cultivation of contextual learning through content awareness, assessment, and application
Learner With Learner Collaboration	Advanced[b]	Contextually based problem solving and decision making

[a]The instructor-learner relationship often serves as the lens through which the learner develops a relationship with the instructional content. Although learners commonly have varying degrees of experience with content, positive instructor-learner relationships enable learners to expand their relationship with the content.

[b]Learners collaborate most effectively when they have engaged in contextual learning and possess a working relationship with the instructional content.

With traditional instruction, the teacher relies upon face-to-face oral communications reinforced with written communications to initiate and sustain critical instructional relationships. Although traditional instruction may foster the development of instructional relationships, it does not guarantee that these vital relationships will form. In online instruction, without benefit of face-to-face oral and body language or nonverbal communications, the instructor must (a) creatively use text and multimedia to advantage and (b) capitalize upon the potential of online communication for fostering necessary instructional relationships.

Communication in Online Instruction

Figure 3.2 illustrates the three phases of *online instructional communication*. As with traditional instructional communication, online instructional communication involves *input*, *process*, and *output*. In traditional instructional communication, instructor and learner primarily use face-to-face in-class communications as opportunities for message clarification. In online instructional communication, text-based or written communications are used to clarify or provide feedback about content. If elements of instruction are confusing, the learner and the instructor may interact *prior to*, *during*, and *after* the learner processes content information. Electronic mail, video messaging, discussion, and chat capabilities enable frequent communications between instructor and learner and between or among learners. As learning technologies become more diverse and sophisticated, face-to-face oral communications should become more prevalent in online instruction.

A major implication for teachers and trainers who aspire to teach online is that they must possess or acquire excellent written communication skills. Effective written communication skills allow instructors to share complete, concise, and clear messages that minimize miscommunications. Teachers and trainers need to develop skills in using learning technologies as communication tools.

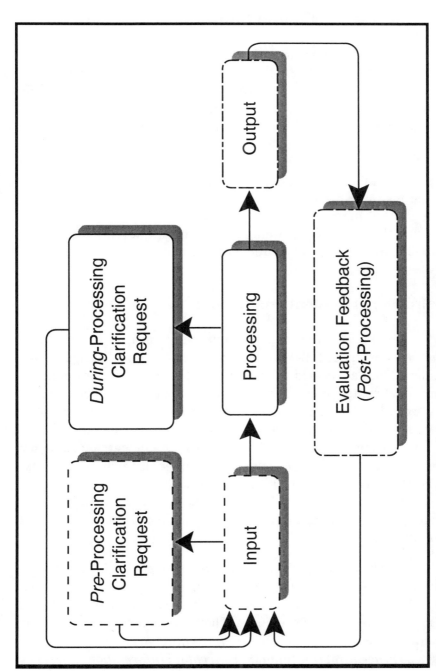

Figure 3.2. Three phases of online instructional communication.

Migration to
Online Instruction

Teachers and trainers should avoid the unnecessary pressure of interpreting online instruction to mean *an all-or-nothing proposition*. Movement or transition from traditional instruction to online instruction usually involves incremental migration. Infrequently do instructors move immediately from traditional instruction to online instruction. Rather, existing traditionally taught content is converted into formats conducive for online delivery. Paul (1999) expounded at length on the concept that there is no one-size-fits-all model for online instruction. In addition to the content undergoing a conversion process, preparations must be made for presenting the content in a virtual classroom or learning environment. The participants must also prepare to interact with the content and with one another in a new environment.

Instructional Content Preparation

As with traditional instruction, online instruction should be soundly constructed following a workable instructional design model. Snider (2000) advocated consideration of five criteria for online instructional content preparation. These include (a) type of content, (b) frequency of change in content, (c) frequency of content access by users, (d) variety of user types and styles, and (e) availability of technology to support content delivery. Notably, content standards are needed. The design and development of online instruction can be expensive. Costs associated with each of these criteria must be weighed against the benefits to be derived, and an infrastructure including technical support is needed during online instructional content design and development.

Hackos and Stevens (1997) recommended that instructors determine stages of learner use ranging from novice to expert performer and whether or not the content must support each stage of learner use or multiple stages in one audience. They also suggest that instructors determine the categories of learner *information needs*, whether learners need *procedural information*, *conceptual information*, *reference information,* or ***hybrid information***, which combines procedural and conceptual information that encourages comprehensive learning experiences. Generic guidelines for presenting these kinds of information are as follows:

Procedural Information Guidelines

✗ Include user-based tasks.

✗ Show the big picture.

✗ Include only procedures appropriate for online presentation.

✗ Include simple purpose statements.

✗ Tell users what to do.

✗ Provide definitions that help learners complete online tasks.

Conceptual Information Guidelines

✗ Tell the learners only what they need to know.

✗ Write abstracts that explain the content and purpose of conceptual information.

✗ Provide enough information for all stages of use among learners who need conceptual information.

✗ Provide information topics that.

    ✗ Help learners grasp why they might want to follow a particular course of action

    ✗ Enable learners to make decisions

    ✗ Help learners grasp necessary technical theory

    ✗ Include typical scenarios learners might follow to achieve a goal

✗ Provide definitions of terms to increase comprehension.

✗ Include information about the authors, if pertinent.

✗ Provide publication dates for all information in the information system.

Reference Information Guidelines

✗ Provide information that will be used repeatedly, or rarely.

✗ Provide discrete pieces of data that will promote comprehension and enable decision making.

Hybrid Information Guidelines

✗ Enable learners to actually complete a task while following procedures.

✗ Use relevant and easy-to-understand illustrations.

✗ Include simulation exercises to allow practice in a safe environment.

✗ Provide constructive feedback.

✗ Use demonstrations to show how a procedure works.

✗ Give learners tools to build contexts, skills, and capacity to learn.

Across-the-board guidelines for mixing information types presented within online instruction include (a) considering the learners needs, (b) analyzing sources of available information, (c) avoiding use of paper-based information to back up all electronically conveyed information, and (d) purposefully deciding how to combine information types.

Driven by concern for the integrity or quality of instructional content delivered online, many professions and organizations invest in the development and updating of position statements, policies, procedures, and protocol conventions for regulating the preparation of instructional content for online delivery. Local guidelines may govern legal and ethical uses of resources in online instruction.

The Commission for Business and Economic Education's (1999) *This We Believe About Distance Learning in Business Education Policy Statement* is a good example of professional organizations providing guidance for development of online instruction. The Distance Education Clearinghouse (2000) also provides current practice and trend information about online instructional content design, development, implementation, and evaluation. Snider (2000) emphasized that individual instructors are ultimately responsible for determining appropriate online uses of instructional content. Their primary challenge is to make online instruction meaningful, engaging, and as interactive as effective face-to-face instruction. Effective communication skills, particularly writing skills, are integral to meeting this challenge.

Learning Environment Preparation

Traditional instruction customarily occurs in a room or space within a building or facility or in some designated place, commonly referred to as a learning environment. Many of the same considerations are taken into account when preparing an online learning environment as for a traditional learning environment, because *an online learning environment is, in a sense, a virtual facility*. Salisbury (1996) encouraged replacement of the concept of classroom with its rows of seats and desks with something that resembles a contemporary electronic work environment. Example considerations include attending to environmental or facility health factors, providing accessibility to necessary resources and tools, and creating appropriate work patterns and habits for participation in the environment.

Instructors preparing to teach in an online environment are encouraged to think about the overarching environment in which their learning environments reside. Will online instruction occur within a Web site? a course management system? or in some other configuration? What are the macro and micro factors likely to affect an online learning environment? Answers to these questions grow out the learning environment's intended functionality and how it is structured to serve general and specific instructional purposes. Also important is the designation of common areas within the instructional environment. These are areas in which learners can frequently congregate or through which they frequently journey. The nature and characteristics of the learners also affect the environment. Instructors need to know their students and to understand the environment needed for students to learn efficiently.

Both traditional and online learning environments depend upon supportive infrastructures. The infrastructure of an online learning environment should be structured to accommodate access for and participation of the targeted learners. The design of an online learning environment, as a virtual facility, should allow users to enter freely and to move about. The environment should be safe, secure for use, supportive of learning, and arranged in a manner supportive of functionality, communication, and engagement. Periodic servicing constitutes a critical dimension of any learning environment infrastructure. Instructors preparing to teach online need to determine what foundational support services help grow a healthy infrastructure. Examples include (a) the technical support required by the instructor and learners and (b) the policies, processes, and practices by which instructional content is delivered and consumed, and by which learning is assessed. The University of Tennessee, Department of Human Resource Development, *HRD Online Gateway* (2000) illustrates how one organization attends to instructor and learner technical support requirements.

The pivotal question—*How does the learning environment's infrastructure promote instructional relationship building?*—needs to be asked and answered on an ongoing basis. Ideally, a learning environment's infrastructure is operational prior to actual instruction. A properly functioning infrastructure helps the instructor and the learner stay abreast of the learning environment's resource base and aids the instructor in his or her acquaintance and ongoing familiarity with what resources are needed to actualize the instructional mission.

A perpetually healthy, growing, and renewing learning environment is impossible without a sound infrastructure. Almost any element in an online learning environment can affect learners' and instructors' well-being in the environment. Major strategies for cultivating a healthy online learning environment are

    ✗ Obtaining feedback on a regular, ongoing basis from learners about the learning environment, its infrastructure, and the intentions or purposes of instructional content and related learner performance expectations

✗ Benchmarking models of healthy learning environments and their infrastructures

✗ Committing to cultivate the learning environment's infrastructure as the foundational base for learning success

According to the North Carolina Department of Public Instruction (1999), teachers responsible for designing and managing technology-intensive learning environments and resources need advanced technology competencies.

These include demonstration of the following skill sets:

1. Develop performance tasks that require students to

   (a) locate and analyze information as well as draw conclusions and

   (b) use a variety of media to communicate results clearly.

2. Use computers and other technologies effectively and appropriately to collect information on student's learning using a variety of methods.

3. Use computers and other technologies effectively and appropriately to communicate information in a variety of formats on student learning to colleagues, parents, and others; and demonstration of these skill sets through practical application.

4. Develop physical settings that support active student involvement, inquiry, and collaboration.

5. Employ organizational and management strategies that support student involvement, inquiry, and collaboration.

6. Use available resources including satellite, cable wireless, and ITFS.

7. Select and create learning experiences that are appropriate for curriculum goals, are relevant to learners, are based upon principles of effective teaching and learning, incorporate the use of media and technology for teaching where appropriate, and support learner expression in a variety of media using diverse media communication tools.

Participant Preparation

The preparation of primary participants in online instruction involves preparation of instructors and preparation of learners.

Preparing the Instructor. Fear keeps many teachers and trainers from exploring the potential of online instruction. From an instructional perspective, fear of the unknown, fear of change, and fear of failure pose major barriers to online instructional success. People evolve, as do organizations, at varying rates. The inclination and readiness to teach online often relate to whether one has access to requisite resources such as release time for online instructional content design and development or adequate tools.

According to Sitze (2000), online teaching requires a new set of teaching skills, including (a) ability to build a personal connection with students whom the teacher may never meet in person and (b) ability to convey and strategically use humor. Other important pre-requisites entail being able to write clearly focused messages, to provide clear expectations of student responsibilities, and to cope with the imperfect science and art of teaching in a dynamic electronic arena. Determining instructional content standards, learner performance assessment, and teaching effectiveness assessment are additional challenges for online teachers and trainers.

Online instruction provides rich opportunities for mentoring. Skills such as online coaching and mentoring are best honed through practical online experience. Also important is the instructor's ability to serve as both manager and conservationist of the online learning environment. Although not solely responsible for the in-frastructure of this environment, the instructor must have a sense of what is appropriate and needed to have a balanced online facility in which to teach.

Preparing the Learner. When interviewed about online learning, Negroponte (2000), well-known author of *Being Digital*, shared, "The highest priority is to make sure the user feels fully in control . . . people make the mistake of thinking of the consumer as a destination point" (p.14). Salisbury (1996) recommended allowing students to change roles from that of passive recipients of information to active information workers. (This means students can access appropriate information and use it to write reports, draw conclusions, or solve problems.) Consistent with Negroponte and Salisbury's observations, Figure 3.3 shows how online instruction fosters a fundamental shift in the roles of instructor and learner. Note that in traditional instructor-led learning, the instructor occupies the role of leader and wields more weight in the learning process. By contrast, in online learner-led learning, the student is allowed and expected to be more self-directed. When properly facilitated by the instructor, self-directed learners can expand their capacity for learning how to learn and for understanding the dynamics of just-in-time learning and supply-and-demand–based interactions. However, on a cautionary note, students unaccustomed to self-directing their own learning may not be qualified to direct their learning. Some may need assistance and training in becoming self-directed, whereas others may never have baseline ability to succeed in a self-directed instructional situation. Consequently, online learning may not be suitable for all types of learners.

Online resources, such as those produced by Pennsylvania State University World Campus (2000), are available for assisting students in gearing up for learning online. Gale (2000) urged students to acquire (a) the necessary computer skills, (b) the necessary hardware requirements, and (c) the necessary software requirements for participating in online instruction.

Salisbury (1996) indicated that as technology increases, learning in school facilities may take on less and less importance. Electronic learning resources and the entire technology of the emerging information infrastructure will make learning better, faster, and cheaper; and will allow students to learn easily at home or in a variety of other individual or group settings.

Summary

Online instruction, the instructional text- and multimedia-based presentation formats used in a web-based delivery system, is

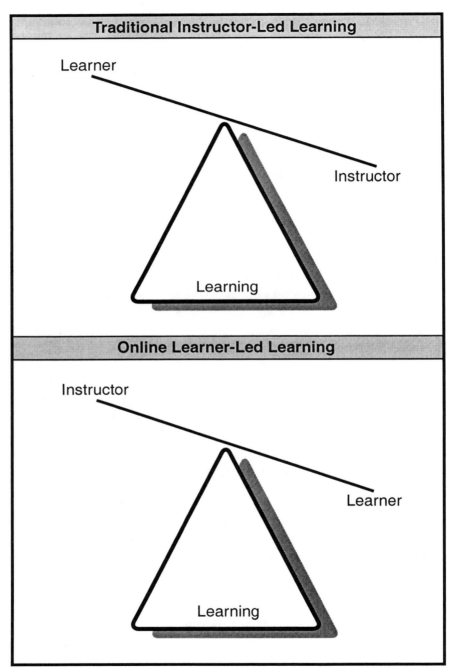

Figure 3.3. Fundamental shift in the roles of instructor and learner.

becoming more prevalent in both the private and public sectors of contemporary society. Facilitation of online instructional relationship building emanates from effective online instructional communication. As teachers and trainers prepare to offer online instruction, they must develop and refine their abilities to write, use learning technologies as communication tools, prepare appropriate online instructional content, prepare an online learning environment with a healthy infrastructure, and prepare themselves and learners for online success.

References

Commission for Business and Economic Education. (1999). *This we believe about distance learning in business education (Policy Statement 65)*. Alexandria, VA: National Business Education Association.

Distance Education Clearinghouse. (2000). *Today's distance education headlines, journals, bibliographies and other readings* [Online]. Available: http://www.uwex.edu/disted.home.html (accessed: June 2000).

Gale, C. (2000, January). Online learning: A student perspective. *Syllabus, 13,* 52-53.

Hackos, J. T., & Stevens, D. M. (1997). *Standards for online communication: Publishing information for the Internet and World Wide Web, corporate intranets, and help systems.* New York: John Wiley & Sons.

McMurrer, D., Van Buren, M., & Woodwell, W. (2000). *The 2000 ASTD state of the industry report.* Alexandria, VA: American Society for Training & Development.

Negroponte, N. (2000). News & comment, up close, being even more digital. *Inside Technology Training, 4,* 14.

North Carolina Department of Public Instruction. (1999). *Technology competencies, advanced technology competencies, design and management of learning environments/resources* [Online]. Available: http://www.unca.edu/education/edtech/competencies/ (accessed: July 2000).

Paul, L. (1999). One size doesn't fit all. *Inside Technology Training. 3*, 30-32, 34, 36.

Pennsylvania State University World Campus. (2000). *Course in how to learn online* [Online]. Available: http://www.worldcampus. psu.edu:8900/public/wc101/ (accessed: July 2000).

Piskurich, G. (1998). Future forces. In G. Piskurich & E. Sanders (Eds.), *ASTD models for learning technologies, roles, competencies, and outputs* (pp. 5-6). Alexandria, VA: American Society for Training & Development.

Piskurich, G., & Sanders. E. (Eds.). (1998). *ASTD models for learning technologies, roles, competencies, and outputs.* Alexandria, VA: American Society for Training & Development.

Salisbury D. (1996). *Five technologies for educational change.* Englewood Cliffs, NJ: Educational Technology Publications.

Sitze, A. (2000). Teachers at a distance. *Inside Technology Training, 4*, 40-42, 44-45.

Snider, A. (2000). A short primer on thinking about online education. *E-learning 1*, 42-43.

The University of Tennessee, Department of Human Resource Development. (2000). *HRD Online Gateway* [Online]. Available: http://web.utk.edu/T7Edavidh/gateway2/enter.htm (accessed: July 2000).

CHAPTER 4
FACILITATING ONLINE LEARNING

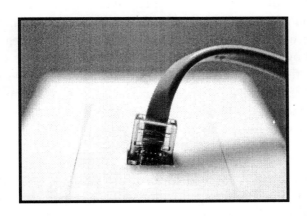

The instructor directs the process for online learning by the selection of materials and activities for the learner. The literature says we retain 10% of what we read, 20% of what we hear, 30% of what we see, 50% of what we hear and see, 70% of what we say , and 90% of what we say and do (Pike, 1994, p.77). This being the case, we have the opportunity in methods selection to increase student retention for online learning by using multimedia. Pike's ADA approach can start one thinking about the types of experiences possible. He suggests the learner first do an Activity, then Discuss it and finally Apply it. This guide can be applied as you select methods from the following sections of content delivery for the activity, interaction methods for the discussion, and application methods for applying the learning.

The main difference in online learning and the traditional programmed instruction is that online instruction can offer opportunities for group interaction. In some respects, online learning can be considered a form of programmed instruction, self-learning using the computer to attain a specific level of performance. The choice of materials is the most important hurtle to preparing an effective program.

Online learning can also be closely related to traditional directed study when directed study is defined as reading selected theory and factual material in a controlled situation and under the direction and guidance of a leader or teacher. Online teaching includes the presentation of information and then checking to see if the facts and knowledge contained in that information have been learned. The online setting may have the learner respond to quiz or discussion questions after completing the lesson. In such cases, the instructor checks and responds, providing a direct acknowledgement of correct or incorrect answers with prompts for encouraging the learner to continue.

The instructor facilitates the learning by the selection of content and techniques for learning. Some educational experts use prescriptions for teaching facts, concepts, interpersonal skills, and attitudes (Kemp, Morrison, & Ross, 1998). These enable the teacher to select techniques that are compatible with the educational outcomes. In applying this concept, as presented in Figure 4.1, to online learning, we will guide you through a three-step process.

Step 1—Educational Outcomes

Decide on the *educational outcomes* for the material to be taught and then select appropriate instructional techniques. The checklist provided in Figure 4.2, titled "Instructional Methods for Educational Outcomes," will facilitate this process.

Step 2—Selection of Instructional Techniques

To aid in your *selection of instructional techniques,* review the characteristics of each as shown in Figure 4.3. The figure shows the selections for content delivery methods, interaction methods, and

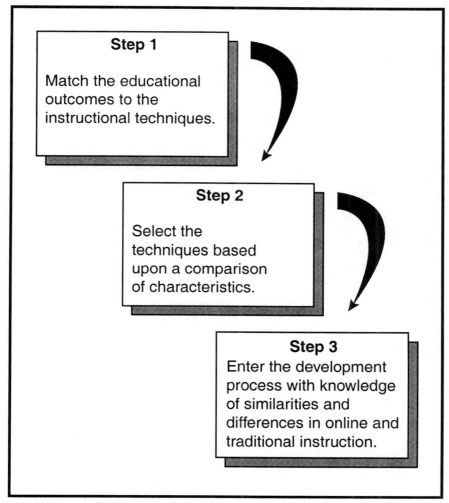

Figure 4.1. The instructor as a facilitator of learning.

application methods. Depending upon the educational outcomes desired as selected in Figure 4.2, the instructor may select the method of content delivery and also some type of interaction activity for the learner to process the information. Finally, if desired or if the content lends itself to application, the instructor selects methods that allow the learner to use the information in a controlled setting.

	Content Delivery			Interaction		Application		
	Lecture	Demonstration	Panel	Group Discussion	Questioning	Role Playing	Case Study	Simulation
Cognitive Outcomes								
Information	X	X	X	X	X	X	X	X
Comprehension	X	X	X	X	X	X	X	X
Application			X	X	X	X	X	X
Analysis				X	X	X	X	X
Synthesis				X	X	X	X	X
Evaluation		X			X	X	X	X
Skill Outcomes								
Imitation		X			X			X
Initiation					X	X	X	X
Mastery							X	X
Attitude Outcomes								
Receiving	X		X					
Responding				X	X	X	X	X
Valuing				X	X	X	X	X
Organizing							X	X

Figure 4.2. Instructional methods for educational outcomes.

Process	Pro(s)	Con(s)	Applications
Content Delivery Methods			
Lecture	Efficient for delivery of content	Major responsibility on instructor; limited for long-term retention	Presenting material to all sizes of groups
Demonstration	Allows first-hand visualization of a process Supports integration of theory with practice	Can be time intensive to prepare	Illustration of processes involving multiple steps
Panel	Multiple views on a topic may be presented	Difficult to organize	Promotes understanding of different parts of a topic
Interaction Methods			
Group Discussion	Promotes understanding	Time-consuming	Taking the content to higher cognitive levels
Questioning	Can foster development of higher order thinking skills	Can become tangential if managed improperly	Promotes problem solving and decision making by individuals and groups
Application Methods			
Role-Playing	Allows for "safe" portrayal of behaviors	Can be expensive to produce	Illustration of interactions and transactions
Case Study	Develops responsibility on part of participants	Time-consuming	Allows participants to apply content and experience
Simulation	Enables "safe" practice with expensive and potentially dangerous processes and resources	Can be expensive to design and develop	Fosters travel across time and space

Figure 4.3. A comparison of characteristics of instructional methods.

Content Delivery Methods: Online Versus Traditional	
Similarities	**Differences**
Delivers content to all size audiences	Cannot see audience's reaction; need to build in ways to allow for questioning
Uses one-way communication	Can add outside points of interest for participant involvement
Requires systematic preparation with attentiveness to detail and cohesiveness	Once prepared can be updated easily
	Can be repeated by the participant at any time
	Is introduced or launched using written communication

Interaction Methods: Online versus Traditional	
Similarities	**Differences**
Allows the participant to become involved in understanding the content	May take a longer time for the group to become comfortable working together because of the online and not in-person interaction
Fosters higher levels of cognitive outcomes	Course management tools allow instructor to track individual involvement in an activity
Group work can be unequal if some participants are not as involved	Predominantly conducted using written communication
Requires intensive reflection and preparation to conduct effect	

Application Methods: Online versus Traditional	
Similarities	**Differences**
Time involved in the organization and set up of the activity	Calls for creative methods to use some activities online
Higher level of application and learning	Can track individual involvement in an activity
Staged to show relatedness to theory and research	Requires meticulous working of performance expectations/requirements

Figure 4.4. Online versus traditional instruction.

Step 3—Similarities and Differences in Online and Traditional Instruction

These methods may sound exactly like traditional classroom methods. However, there are **similarities and differences in online and traditional instruction** (Figure 4.4). It is important to understand these similarities and differences to be comfortable in using them. Before you begin reading about each technique, you will be using this quick review that highlights these points.

While approaching the mechanics of selecting learning experiences, it is important to remember **the teacher is more than a learning organizer**. Wittmer and Myrick (1989) discuss six characteristics of a facilitative teacher. **Facilitative teachers are attentive, genuine, understanding, respectful, knowledgeable, and communicative.** Always remember, these characteristics are just as important when teaching online.

References

Kemp, J. E., Morrison, G. R., & Ross, S. M. (1998). *Designing effective instruction.* Upper Saddle River, NJ: Prentice Hall.

Pike, R. W. (1994). *Creative training techniques handbook.* Minneapolis, MN: Lakewood Books.

Wittmer, J., & Myrick, R. D. (1989). *The teacher as facilitator.* Minneapolis, MN: Educational Media Corporation.

PART II
CONTENT DELIVERY METHODS

CHAPTER 5
CONTENT DELIVERY: LECTURE

CHAPTER 6
CONTENT DELIVERY: DEMONSTRATION

CHAPTER 7
CONTENT DELIVERY: PANEL

CHAPTER 5
Content Delivery: Lecture

Definition

The lecture is a method of presenting facts, information, and principles. It is one way to present content to learners. In this manner, the content delivery is often the first part of a complete lesson. The online lecture may be delivered in several ways including taped audio or video, written text or outline, or combinations of these.

Introduction

The lecture is a traditional teaching method that has been criticized because it provides no opportunity for the audience to participate in the presentation. Telling people what you want them to know, however, is still one of the most common methods of teaching. The online lecture, however, requires some participation to access the information. The interaction can be as basic as activating a video or audio clip that is part of the online presentation or taking a side journey to a Web site to gain the information selected by the instructor.

When lecturing, the expert in the field gives an organized, in-depth presentation to the audience. It is a convenient method for presenting a large amount of information to an audience in a relatively short time. One measure of effectiveness of delivering content described by the American Society for Training and Development (ASTD) (Bedrosian, 1995) is examining the message to detertmine its value, clarity, logic, and good delivery and to see if it is memorable, understandable, realistic, and challenging. Online lectures can measure up to these characteristics.

Online lectures have several advantages. The most obvious is the flexibility of receiving the lecture at a convenient time. Many instructors teaching online are not at all surprised to view the course management statistics and to see the majority of the students are online after 9:00 p.m. Other advantages include being able to replay the lecture at anytime and to take more time with complicated aspects of the presentation.

Main Procedural Steps in Using the Lecture

First, be certain you have selected the best technique for the level of learning you expect of the participant. If you want to INPUT CONTENT to increase learners' knowledge or understanding, you have selected the best technique. If you want the participant to go beyond this to analysis, synthesis, or application of the content, you may wish to start here but add an experience from other areas of this book to complete your lesson.

The procedure for using the lecture technique begins with careful preparation. For the lecture technique to be effective, the presenter must know his or her subject matter. Once the presenter is prepared, the lecture must be organized and developed to prepare the manner of presentation to the audience in a way that will keep them interested and get the material across clearly. To do this, take the following steps.

Step 1—Outline Your Presentation

There are no walk-in lectures in online learning. Expect to spend time in preparation of the material. Every good lecture begins with a good outline. Once it is developed, you can add, refine, and update, but it should be available for students to see and study— and it should represent your best work.

The outline not only will keep you focused during the development stage but also will provide a good checkpoint for learners. Remember in the beginning to draw attention to the content. Then state and restate major concepts to clarify your points. Share your outline through the lecture by describing the points you are going to cover and what expectations you have for their learning (Figure 5.1).

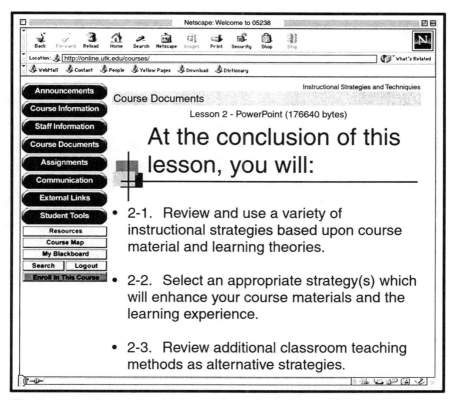

Figure 5.1. Example of lesson outline using learner expectations.

Then keep your points or course objectives in order as you progress. Finally, keep the outline simple so it doesn't become a distraction.

Step 2—Keep It Simple

In online course development, you should develop a pattern of telling the audience what they will learn in a similar way for each lecture. That will accustom them to tuning in on the important aspects of what will follow. Figure 5.2 is an example of the selected content one group of faculty developing undergraduate online courses follows for consistency.

Element	Online Position Within Course Management System
Annoucement	At opening of course site or gateway
Course ID	On first screen of each lesson
Lesson ID (Title)	As first element on each lesson
Lesson Objective	As second element on each lesson
Lesson Summary	As next-to-last element of each lesson
Lesson Assignment	As last element of each lesson

Figure 5.2. Example of guidelines for online lesson preparation.

It is a good idea to let the learners know up front what their responsibilities are. Included here would be completing the readings, visiting any sites incorporated into the lecture, and/or viewing or listening to any clips.

Most audiences can only absorb a few main ideas at each sitting. Generally, two to four main ideas should be the maximum presented during a lecture. Although the concepts can be complicated, the structure of the lecture should be kept simple.

A good start can set the tone for the whole lecture. It also helps to establish the purpose of the lecture both in your mind and in the mind of the learners. The introduction should be carefully planned and as interesting as possible.

Audiences listen better and retain more when they know what to watch for and what the purpose is. Spell out your objectives at the beginning. Repeat them at the end. Figure 5.3 shows the summary used at the end of the lesson. This is a restatement in summary form of the objectives shown in Figure 5.1. Repetition is important for retention. Important points need to be repeated at least three times in order to be remembered.

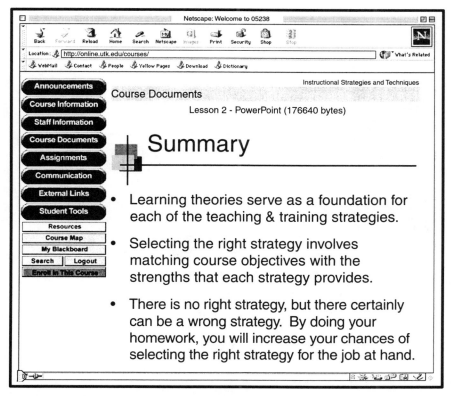

Figure 5.3. Example of the lesson summary repeating the learner expectations.

Step 3—Use a Conversational Approach

Conversational style is important to the lecture process. The conversational approach can be useful for online learning. Your personality will show through (see Figure 5.4). Therefore add your comments to material presented; put yourself into the notes and material you prepare. Don't think that because you are not there in person your audience should not get to know you. You can do this in any number of ways. You may want to have a regular sidebar approach with your picture and a direct quote from you as a comment on the content presented. A video clip of you can also be inserted where you illustrate the points "in person" as a part of the lecture. Sometimes your selection of cartoons or graphics to illustrate points can reflect your personality.

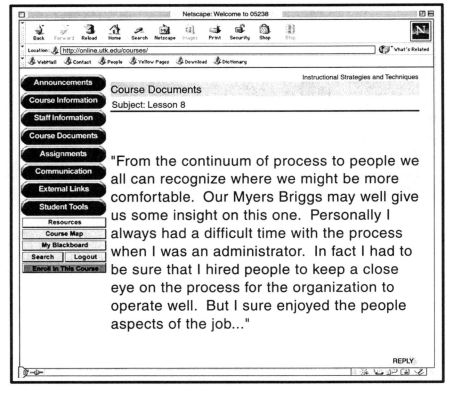

Figure 5.4. Example of conversational text.

The presenter should know his or her audience and tailor the lecture to their level. This includes avoiding unfamiliar words and stiff formality. Brewer and Traver (1978) support using humor, anecdotes, and visual aids to help keep the audience alert and involved in the lecture process. Just as you do this in person, you can add a similar tone and keep the learner engaged while online.

The presenter should arrange the material so that ideas are expressed clearly. Be specific; use short sentences for emphasis. Terms such as *however, nevertheless, then* and *finally* are important transitions online just as they are in person.

Step 4—Vary Your Presentation

Audience interest and retention depends in part upon how well the material is presented. Avoid using one technique exclusively. Integrate outlining major points with commentary and some audio and video presentation for emphasis and variety (Kemp, Morrison, & Ross, 1998). Often you can find excellent Web sites as in Figure 5.5 for presentation of ideas or reinforcement of the content. Your comments about the site and what it is intended for are important.

Step 5—Show Enthusiasm

An appropriate level of enthusiasm conveys the presenter's attitude toward the subject matter. If the presenter demonstrates a high level of enthusiasm, the audience will tap into this energy and be encouraged to listen. How can you show enthusiasm online? Change the print, change the color, add a cartoon, have the learner click on an icon that reveals something special or that transmits your voice emphasizing the point.

Step 6—Take the Content a Step Further

The pure lecture can present content effectively and can be made interesting by the variations you add. However, it will be greatly enhanced by taking it a step further. Brookfield (1990) suggests that

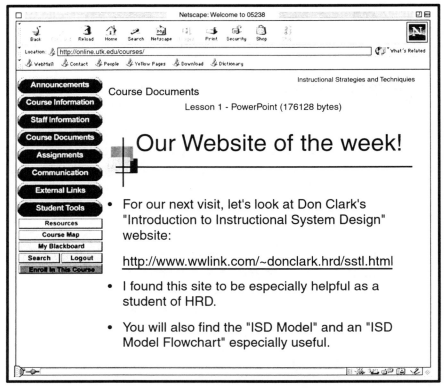

Figure 5.5. Example of a Website reinforcing content.

a way to spark interest is to end the lecture with a question related to the topic to initiate a thought-provoking free flow of ideas among individuals within a group. Online lecturing can lead to a linear relationship between the teacher and the student. The teacher prepares information for the student, and the student performs based upon his or her interaction with the material. If it ends here, there is no feedback allowing for clarification and leading to higher levels of learning. There are ways feedback can be built into the lecture to create a circular relationship of learning. The lecturer can build in questions that a live audience would have asked and then work the answers into the material presented. This questioning can stimulate thinking and keep the learner's interest. It is only a simulated feedback, but experienced instructors can make good use of realistic questions.

The sections of this book on interaction and application will provide you with many ideas on how to create this atmosphere for follow-up on the lecture content. Remember, interactive discussion and other application activities allow the learners to clarify and retain the material.

Variations of the Lecture

As the author of the lecture, you will decide on the **format** of the material to be presented and the additions of **illustrative material** and the **media** to be used for delivery.

Format

The content you present may be an **original text** in which you have a great deal of reading online for the learner. When this is the case, you should look for ways to emphasize points within the text, add visuals, and keep learners' interest.

At times, you will present the lecture in an **outline** format using supportive text as a reference. Your content will emphasize the main points of the text and add your original thoughts.

You could select the **audio or video** format for presentation of the lecture. If this is your choice, be sure that learners have access to the necessary software for downloading and that you have formatted the material for the best and most efficient use. Streaming audio and video and free access to software that allows viewing is being made more available and easier to use.

These formats do not have to be used exclusively. In fact, when more than one is selected for use in the same presentation or in a series of lectures that make up a course, they keep the learners interest and add variety that stimulates learning. One of Robert Pike's (1994) "Laws of Adult Learning" is "Learning is directly proportional to the amount of fun you have" (p. 4). Overuse of one of the lecture formats can become boring and you will quickly lose learners' attention. Interjecting different lecture formats can be fun for the learner and for the presenter.

Illustrative Material

The inclusion of illustrations such as drawings, cartoons, graphics, pictures, and videos is as important online as in person. The audiovisual adds a helpful learning style or aid to the lecture method. Brewer, Hollingsworth, and Campbell (1995) and Parker (1993) suggest that lectures should use visual imagery that ties in with the words in the lecture so the viewer can retrieve a mental picture of the subject to reinforce learning. Figure 5.6 is an example of using pictures to make a point.

The reasons for carefully designing and using visuals are also similar to some of those for in-person lectures:

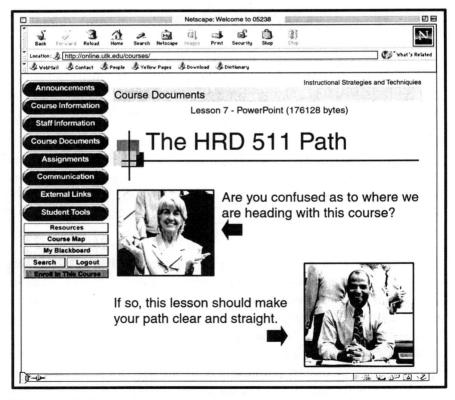

Figure 5.6. Example of using pictures to help make a point.

1. Attract and maintain attention.
2. Reinforce ideas.
3. Illustrate and support ideas.
4. Clarify meaning.
5. Increase retention.
6. Add realism. (Adapted from Pike, 1994)

As you select or develop these illustrations, make sure they serve a purpose and are compatible with the objectives you have for the learner. They should add and not detract from your content.

Medium

The use of a text format using HTML formatting tools will give you an easy flow of ideas and allow you to interject other formats along the way. Another commonly used format is that of Power Point™ slides that are a part of the lecture or make up the lecture completely. This can be easier for the instructor as a transition to online material preparation. Figures 5.7 and 5.8 illustrate an example of the same content prepared for PowerPoint™ and HTML formats.

Advantages, Disadvantages, and Limitations of the Lecture

When using the lecture instructional strategy, the instructor should be aware of the following advantages, disadvantages, and limitations of this technique (Brewer, 1997).

Advantages of Lecture

1. Require little prior participant knowledge about subject matter.
2. Material can be presented rapidly and logically.
3. Convenient for groups of any size.
4. Directions can be given clearly, therefore ensuring that all participants have the necessary information.

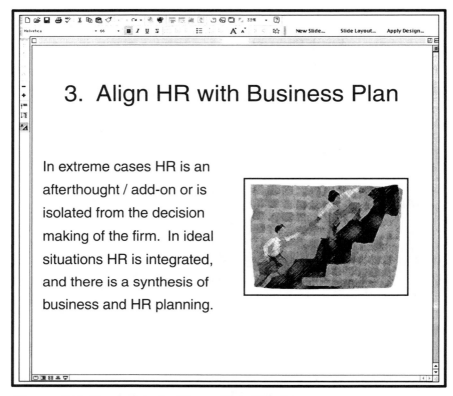

Figure 5.7. Example of a PowerPoint™ slide.

    5. Easier for presenter to coordinate and control.

Disadvantages of Lecture

1. The audience is less likely to retain a large percentage of the material.
2. Overuse of lectures that are too long can lead to boredom on part of audience.
3. The possibility of miscommunication is greater.
4. Reflective thinking on the part of the audience is not encouraged.

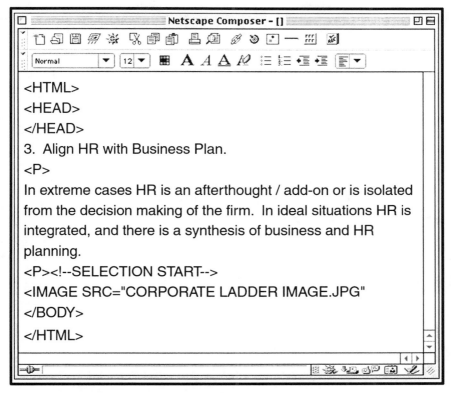

Figure 5.8. Example of material prepared for HTML format.

5. Henson (1993) states that lectures are the least effective teaching method to promote long-term retention.

Limitations of Lecture

1. Not appropriate for hands-on type of skill training

2. Limited feedback from the audience

3. Puts responsibility for material on the presenter

4. Difficult to evaluate

5. Not appropriate for abstract, complex, or highly detailed material

Summary

A lecture should be kept short and interesting, the presenter should have a concrete knowledge of the subject matter, and the presentation should be well organized. When used properly, the lecture can be an effective teaching tool. It is most successful when used informally and enhanced by other methods, such as audiovisual aids and in conjunction with techniques for interaction and application. Gilstrap and Martin (1975) note the range for the lecture method by noting that the lecture can "challenge the imagination of each student, arouse curiosity, develop his [or her] spirit of inquiry, and encourage his [or her] creativity" (p. 7).

References

Bedrosian, M. (1995). *How to make a large group presentation.* Alexandria, VA: American Society for Training and Development.

Brewer, E. W. (1997). *13 proven ways to get your message across: The essential reference for teachers, trainers, presenters, and speakers.* Thousand Oaks, CA: Corwin.

Brewer, E. W., Hollingsworth, C., & Campbell, A. (1995). Accelerated learning and short-term instructional programs: Sustaining interest and intrapersonal growth. *Southeastern Association of Educational Opportunity Program Personnel Journal, 14*(1), 57-85.

Brewer, E. W., & Traver, G. J. (1978). *The funniest jokes.* Bend, OR: Maverick.

Brookfield, S. D. (1990). *The skillful teacher.* San Francisco: Jossey-Bass.

Gilstrap, R. L., & Martin, W. R. (1975). *Current strategies for teachers.* Pacific Palisades, CA: Goodyear.

Henson, K. T. (1993). *Methods and strategies for teaching in secondary and middle schools.* New York: Longman.

Kemp, J. E., Morrison, G. R., & Ross, S. M. (1998). *Designing Effective Instruction.* Upper Saddle River, NJ: Prentice Hall.

Parker, J. K. (1993). Lecturing and loving it. *The Clearing House, 67*(1), 8-10.

Pike, R.W. (1994). *Creative training techniques handbook.* Minneapolis, MN: Lakewood Books.

The Lecture Planning Sheet

Date:_____Time:_____Site:_____

Intended Audience:

Topic Statement:

Objective(s) of Session:

Main Ideas of Lecture:

       1.
       2.
       3.
       4.
       5.

Media Needed:

Handouts:

Follow-Up Activity(ies):

Summary Notes:

The Lecture Evaluation Sheet

(✱You may wish to have someone else consider these items, as well as evaluating yourself.)

✱Was the lecturer's purpose clear?
__Yes __No (Explain)

✱Was the pace appropriate? (slower for difficult material, faster for easier ideas and review) __Yes __No (Explain)

✱Was the lecture delivered in an enthusiastic manner?
__Yes __No (Explain)

✱Were audiovisuals helpful for clarifying or expanding ideas?
__Yes __No (Explain)

Was follow-up activity used?
__Yes (If so, were directions clear?) __No (Explain)

✱What contribution did the follow-up make to the purpose/message of this session?

Did the audience participate enthusiastically?
__Yes __No (Explain)

What was the general level of audience interest?

✱What was especially effective about this session?

✱Suggestions for improvement:

CHAPTER 6
CONTENT DELIVERY:
DEMONSTRATION

Definition

Demonstration is a teaching method for visually presenting and explaining a sequential process or facts and concepts. It requires manipulation on the part of the presenter and observation on the part of the participant. Online instructional demonstrations allow participants to see how a particular task is performed or a problem is solved by watching the presenter perform a process or share the sequential flow and implications of information. Typically, demonstrations include verbal, step-by-step explanations that guide the participants to imitate them later on their own.

Introduction

Online demonstrations commonly involve multimedia and may be synchronous or asynchronous. Common forms of synchronous demonstration include Webcasting, network conferencing, or real-time chatting accompanied by text. Asynchronous demonstrations might consist of CD-ROM files, streamed video, streamed audio accompanied by text, presentation graphics with text, audio and digital photographs, or a series of links that enable participants to step through procedures.

Effective online presenters want to teach dynamic material that is interesting, understandable, and memorable. They realize that participants learn in a variety of ways and that many learners require hands-on experiences. According to Lazear (1991), the demonstration content delivery method appeals to and supports *verbal/linguistic* and *visual spatial* intelligence or learning preferences.

Verbally/linguistically inclined learners relate to written and spoken words and language, and visually or spatially inclined learners rely on sight and on being able to visualize objects. Verbal/linguistic learners respond and are sensitive to semantics (the meanings of words), syntax (the order of words within a context), phonology (the sounds, rhythms, inflection, and meter of words), and praxis (the different uses of words). Presenters aspiring to provide meaningful demonstrations for verbal/linguistic learners should consider and plan for the integrative effect of semantics, syntax, phonology, and praxis. Figure 6.1 illustrates effective use of these elements in text accompanying a demonstration.

For visual or spatial learners, demonstrations not only provide actual viewing of a sequential process or information, but they also aid in the capture or stimulation of mental images. These images aid in the retrieval, use, and adaptation of the demonstrated process or information in future application situations. Figure 6.2 shows written text and a companion graphic used to convey the fourth step in a six-step process.

The demonstration method allows learners to see in visual images the sequence of steps and to obtain a verbal explanation of how each is performed. The United Nations Educational, Scientific and Cultural Organization (1985) says that demonstrations develop

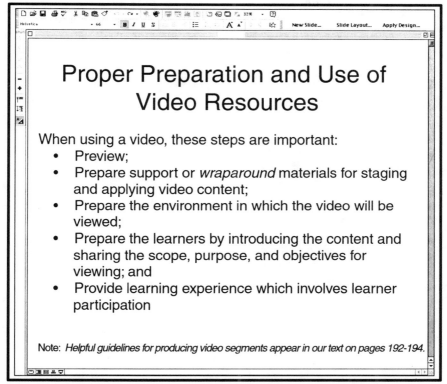

Figure 6.1. Example of demonstraion graphic containing effective semantic, syntax, phonology, and praxis elements.

synchronized cognitive and motor skills, sensory skills, and logical thought patterns.

Main Procedural Steps in Using the Demonstration

The four basic steps of a demonstration are preparation, presentation, application, and testing and follow-up.

Step 1—Preparation

Hackos and Stevens (1997) advise following these guidelines

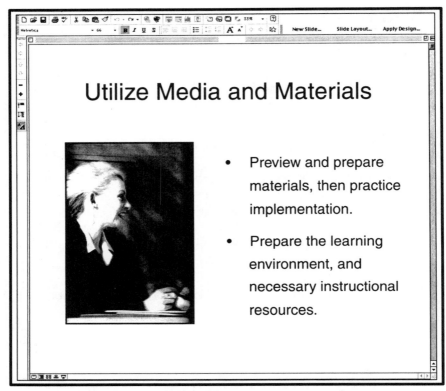

Figure 6.2. Demonstration text and companion graphic.

for shaping the type and sequencing information in procedural top-ics.

    ✗ Include user, not system tasks.

    ✗ Show the big picture.

    ✗ Include only procedures that are appropriate for online pre-sentation.

    ✗ Include simple purpose statements.

    ✗ Tell users what to do.

The presenter should prepare all the information, tools, sup-plies, and equipment before the demonstration. Everything must be accessible and ready to operate at a certain time for the demonstration to be effective. The size of the materials should be taken into account to allow for ample room and should not cause overcrowding or awkward use. The presenter must be sure that an appropriate place has been chosen for staging the demonstration. To prevent potential barriers to the viewing, the presenter should attend to how participants will view the demonstration online. The demonstration should be physically and mentally rehearsed to check for mistakes and to facilitate continuity of ideas. Clermont, Borko, and Krajcik (1994) find that presenters with extensive knowledge base of their subject area and familiarity with their audiences experience the greatest success when using the demonstration as a teaching method. They state that experienced presenters are able to field questions better and to provide mental representations more easily than novices.

There should be a written plan or graphic procedural diagram to follow as a guideline. It should be posted online so participants may access the plan when they are ready to learn this content. The demonstration should be planned around the nature of targeted learners and should vary in length accordingly. Because of potential network congestion and the attention span of learners viewing a demonstration online, special precautions should be taken to limit viewing time required for an online demonstration. Demonstration of a lengthy process might be segmented to enhance online viewing.

Step 2—Presentation

The presentation allows the presenter to describe the different steps, proper procedures, and main ideas of the skill while actually performing the process. Basic vocabulary, short sentences, and familiar words should be used to maintain the attention and understanding of the participants. The presenter should follow an outline to be sure all the steps are performed . He or she should present the information sparingly, one point at a time, to ensure understanding. The presenter should present the information in sequential steps, working from the most basic to the more difficult, paced by the understanding of the participants. The information should be closely related to the procedural steps being performed and should be kept to a minimum with no deviations. While there are many ways to do something, participants should be taught a specific method, and it should be learned thoroughly before another is attempted.

The demonstrator should begin by finding out what knowledge participants already have and relating the new knowledge to that. The demonstration should follow soon after to let the participants know that they too will have a chance to participate. The participants will be more interested in the lesson if they know they will have the chance to use the same equipment or to apply what they have learned on their own in their own way.

Step 3—Application

Application allows the participant to practice what he or she has heard and seen during the presenter's demonstration. A presenter may synchronously or asynchronously monitor the participants' decisions and actions during the application of the demonstrated process or information. Through practice, learners are able to replicate the presenter's previous actions but do the work on their own.

It is important not to take over through suggestions or criticism and remove the participant's sense of importance or responsibility for his or her demonstration. The presenter should point out errors and help the participant think of ways to correct the mistake and then let the participant fix it. Daines (1993) says that it is important to encourage confidence in the participants so they won't be hesitant to participate or perform the demonstration on their own and so they will realize that mistakes will be made and can be corrected.

Step 4—Testing and Follow-Up

The testing step shows whether the participant has understood and mastered the aims of the demonstration to the presenter's satisfaction. Each participant must execute and accomplish the skill the presenter sets before him or her individually. The participant learns for himself or herself the satisfaction and self-confidence of mastering a skill through learning by doing. The testing step is not a time for presenters to offer help but to observe the participant's actions and to help only if there is an emergency. The participant must meet the standards and goals the presenter places before him or her to have mastered the skill.

Variations of the Demonstration

Demonstrations can take many forms. Each method should be appropriate to both the needs of the participant and the objective of the presenter. For example, if the class needs specific instruction in a particular area of electronics, a chalkboard illustration may suffice. An illustrated lecture might correctly address new developments or provide an overview of a particular subject. Text-based materials provide detailed information and drawings on a number of technical and advanced subjects. Also, a sports skill might be properly demonstrated by a coach with a basketball. Each subject determines which method works best.

An example of an online variation of the standard demonstration process is allowing participant involvement within the demonstration. First, the presenter does the demonstration and explains what is happening. Then, synchronously or asynchronously, individuals or groups of participants perform the same operation. When the participants are directly involved, learning is enhanced. With the participant involvement, the presenter is provided with feedback about the success or failure of the demonstration.

An example of another variation is the use of an assistant to aid the presenter in the demonstration. It could be another presenter or an advanced participant. Having someone who is skilled in this area of the demonstration adds practicality and variety.

Penick (1993) suggests a variation on standard demonstration technique in which the participants are given a 1-minute demonstration of a particularly tricky experiment. Then they are given the materials and told to figure out how to reenact the demonstration to have the same results as those of the professor. Penick adds that this variation is mainly useful for stimulating creative thought.

Advantages, Disadvantages, and Limitations of the Demonstration Method

Many times, specific content, such as manipulative skills or scientific theories, is presented in step-by-step processes to ensure understanding and applicability. Demonstration allows participants to show what they have learned and to gain an understanding of the information behind the skill and the reasons for applying the skill. Skill application leads to practice and eventual mastery. Sequential steps help teach participants logical thought patterns for applying a skill or attacking a problem.

Demonstration is used mostly for teaching scientific principles, the movement and relationship of parts of equipment, and hands-on skills. It is used in math, mechanics, practical arts, and vocational and technical education. It is helpful in any instructional setting in which a presenter wants to show participants how to do something.

Participants must try not to fall behind or get lost in the demonstration because a missed step might leave participants confused and with no way to catch up. Demonstrations should be interesting and should have relevance to the participants for them to stay attentive.

When using the demonstration instructional strategy, the presenter should be aware of the following advantages, disadvantages, and limitations of this technique.

Advantages of Demonstration

1. It is a hands-on method of learning.
2. It is effective for visual learners.
3. It is a good way to teach vocational or industrial trades.
4. It teaches participants to think sequentially.
5. Participants are directly involved in their learning.

6. Asynchronous demonstrations are conducive to viewing enactment of a process when access is convenient for the learner.

7. Asynchronous demonstrations may be viewed multiple times, as directed by the learner.

While up-front production costs might be substantial for some online demonstrations, asynchronous demonstrations allow for cost-effective repeated viewing.

Disadvantages of Demonstration

1. Without proper planning or preparation, it is ineffective.

2. If key steps are be skipped, participants will be confused.

3. The length or complexity of the demonstration may lead to boredom and confusion, especially in an online learning environment.

4. Participants might be distracted by content presentation.

5. Slow learners may feel they are in the "spotlight" and may refuse to participate in the replication phase. (Brewer, 1997)

Limitations of Demonstration

1. Network congestion may cause interruptions or delays in viewing and/or accessing a demonstration.

2. Synchronous delivery of a demonstration may be inconvenient for viewing by an entire group of learners.

3. Online multimedia demonstrations require specific hardware and software capabilities for viewing.

4. The demonstration must be timely in terms of participant readiness and relevance to other lessons.

5. The presenter may talk to the materials, not to the participants.

6. Sometimes materials are too costly and substitutes must be used. (Brewer, 1997)

Summary

The demonstration is a rewarding teaching method because, after close observation of the presenter, the participants are able to model the procedure they just witnessed and understand the information surrounding the demonstration. Thus, participants are able to perform the skill afterward, so they learn how and the reasons why. Demonstration provides a stimulating hands-on approach to learning that gives participants a sense of applicability and practicality. Hugo (1993) believes that when participants view demonstrations as relevant to themselves, they are motivated to experience and store the demonstration for future learning or use.

References

Brewer, E. W. (1997). *13 proven ways to get your message across: The essential reference for teachers, trainers, presenters, and speakers.* Thousand Oaks, CA: Corwin.

Clermont, C., Borko, H., & Krajcik, J. (1994). Comparative study of the pedagogical content knowledge of experienced and novice chemical demonstrators. *Journal of Research in Science Teaching, 31*(4), 419-439.

Daines, J. (1993). *Adult learning, adult teaching.* Nottingham, England: Nottingham University, Department of Adult Education. (ERIC Document Reproduction Service No. ED 361 597)

Hackos, J., & Stevens, D. (1997). *Standards for online communication: Publishing information for the Internet/World Wide Web/help systems/corporate intranets.* New York: Wiley Computer Publishing.

Hugo, J. (1993). Combining gases in classes. *Science Teacher, 60*(2), 26-29.

Lazear, D. (1991). *Seven ways of knowing, teaching for multiple intelligences* (2nd ed.). Arlington Heights, IL: IRI SkyLight Training and Publishing.

Penick, J. (1993). The mysterious closed system. *Science Teacher, 60*(2), 30-33.

United Nations Educational, Scientific and Cultural Organization, Division of Science, Technical and Environmental Education. (1985). *A problem-solving approach to environmental education.* Environmental Education Series. Paris: Author. (ERIC Document Reproduction Service No. ED 354 143)

The Demonstration Planning Sheet

Date:_____Recommended Viewing/Accesss Time:_____
Origination Site:_____

Anticipated Composition of Learner Audience:

Title of the Demonstration:

Objective(s) of Session:

Rehearsal Notes:

Relationship to Former Learning:

Demonstration

1. Introduction
2. Procedural steps
3. Statement of results
4. Check for understanding
5. Learner demonstration
6. Check for understanding
7. Other demonstration practices (if this is planned)

Handouts:

Equipment Needs:

Plan for Group Practice (if any):

Summary Notes and Follow-Up (assignment or preview):

The Demonstration Evaluation Sheet

(*You may wish to have someone else consider
these items, as well as evaluating yourself.)

Was the purpose clearly stated? __Yes __No (Explain)

*Did the presenter ascertain and build on participants' prior knowledge?
__Yes __No (Explain)

*Were vocabulary words and terms effectively explained?
__Yes __No (Explain)

*Was the demonstation appropriate for the purpose?
__Yes __No (Explain)

*Did the presenter pace the demonstration for full understanding of the
purpose and the procedure? __Yes __No (Explain)

How effective was this check for understanding?

If the learner was asked to do a demonstration, did this flow well?
__Yes __No (Explain)

Was the presenter supportive so that the learner realized successful
replication of the demonstrated process? __Yes __No (Explain)

Did the learner demonstration serve as a good review of the purpose and
the procedure? __Yes __No (Explain)

Did most participants appear to understand the procedure and the
presenter's expectations before beginning this phase of the session?
__Yes __No (Explain)

*How effective was the monitoring of individual work?

*How helpful were the handouts?

*Were equipment and other materials adequate?
__Yes __No (Explain)

*What was the most effective aspect of the session?

Suggestions for improvement:

CHAPTER 7
CONTENT DELIVERY: PANEL

Definition

A panel is a discussion by a small group of persons, usually three to eight, who present brief lectures on a topic about which they have special knowledge. The panel presents an alternative to a lecture by one person with the opportunity for content to be delivered by a group of experts.

Introduction

The panel, or panel discussion, may be formal or informal, and synchronous or asynchronous. The use of a panel for online instruction or training provides an opportunity to present diverse and possibly controversial ideas. It also can provide reinforcement of the content or illustrate how different people have applied the ideas or content that is being studied.

Main Procedural Steps in Using a Panel

Setting the stage for a panel is quite different when the audience is not physically present. The most important aspect involves preparing the panel members. That requires first deciding the purpose and learning objectives for the panel presentation. If the purpose is clarification of content or application of content presented in lectures or reading material, the interaction of panel members or students may be kept to a minimum. This makes the technology much easier. However if you expect the students to reach higher levels of learning, building in live interaction will be helpful.

The moderator of the panel is responsible for communicating with the panel members the specific questions that should be addressed and the time frame and format for the presentation. Panel members may have the same questions and be videotaped in advance at different times or together. One way to add interaction and questions to a pretaped panel presentation is to build in an online chat or add a discussion board that includes the panelists. Sometimes questions are submitted in advance by audience members and read to the panel by the moderator. During the taping or live broadcast, the moderator is responsible for keeping the discussion moving in the right direction, pulling out points of interest from panel members' lectures, and making sure that all members have a chance to participate equally. This is true when the panel is present at one time or if each member is taped individually.

A skillful panel moderator avoids the biggest pitfalls of panel discussions: keeping the panel members on the topic and clarifying statements made by the panel. Even if the presentation is being taped, for viewing by the student at a later time, the format and the process remain the same.

In the panel discussion, each member of the panel makes statements or presents his or her position. Each panel member is given the same amount of time, and it is up to the moderator to keep the speakers within their allotted time frame. After each panel member has been allowed to speak, the moderator asks for contributions from the audience in the form of questions or comments. When this is done in a synchronous live mode, the lines for chat room communication are opened and panel members respond through the live broadcast or through the chat function.

Usually the time is divided in half, with 20 or 30 minutes allotted to the panel lectures and an equal amount of time dedicated to audience questions and comments. If an asynchronous discussion board is used for questions and comments, the moderator indicates the time frame and format to be used.

The moderator should meet with panel members in advance of the discussion and should introduce panel members to the group at the beginning of the discussion. The moderator should announce the schedule, explain all procedures to the group, and open the panel discussion with a question designed to arouse interest. Following the discussion, the moderator may ask questions to clarify statements. He or she maintains the theme of the discussion.

Variations of the Panel

The panel forum is the only variation of this technique. The pure panel discussion allows for no audience participation. Panel members discuss the subject among themselves, with the moderator preparing questions in advance and adding questions to keep the discussion alive.

A panel forum is a panel discussion that is followed by audience participation in a free and open discussion. Hungerford (1989) says the panel presentation method provides an active learning atmosphere in which participants are encouraged to share their personal opinions and ideologies with others, thus creating a free flow of ideas. The moderator acts as a facilitator between the panel and the audience.

Appropriate Uses, Suggestions, and Cautions

Succcessful use of a panel discussion or panel forum depends on having interesting topics, panelists who are well informed, and a skillful moderator to keep things moving. It is similar to the lecture except that the panelists can present differing points of view.

The panel discussion is appropriate for introducing new materials, motivating students, and summarizing an area of study. It is especially helpful when participants are divided on an issue or have differing opinions. Dienstfrey (1991) suggests using the panel discussion in the form of a game. For instance, the participants become Shakespearean characters from a novel, and the class probes them for information about themselves, thus stimulating the students to learn in a creative, fun way.

Often a panel is used when the discussion of a problem as a whole is too broad in scope. The panel discussion encourages a high level of interaction, especially if the group is involved in the selection of topics. According to the *Instructional Improvement Handbook* (Instructional Improvement Committee, 1992), the panel discussion is also helpful when it involves an outside speaker or panel of speakers who can contribute their knowledge and expertise and spark questions and curiosity from the class.

Advantages, Disadvantages, and Limitations of the Panel

When using the panel instructional strategy, according to Brewer (1997), the teacher should consider the following advantages, disadvantages, and limitations of this technique.

Advantages of the Panel

1. A number of different views on a topic may be presented.
2. Panel members enjoy a high level of freedom to express views or thoughts.

3. Informality can be maintained, allowing for good communication.

4. Different sides of complicated issues can be presented to a large number of people.

Disadvantages of the Panel

1. Panel members frequently stray from the topic.

2. One panel member may monopolize the subject, regardless of whether his or her knowledge is as broad as the other panel members.

3. The audience can become confused by poor panel presentations.

4. If the presentation is not systematic, questions may be left unanswered.

5. Coordination of interaction between students and panel members in an online format is possible but can be technically challenging.

Limitations of the Panel

1. It is difficult to find six to eight panel members who are skillful in discussion and also have a strong knowledge of the subject to be discussed.

2. The panel discussion must be carefully planned, and it may be difficult to get panel members together prior to discussion.

Summary

The panel or panel discussion involves both the audience and a group of people who have a special knowledge about a topic. The panel members can be assigned different points of the topic for discussion and/or can express their opinions on controversial and emotional issues.

The panel has the benefits of the lecture in that a large amount of material can be presented quickly to a large group. In addition, a panel provides the opportunity for a broader variety of ideas on the topic. It can also overcome the lecture's lack of participation by involving the audience if these measures are provided in an online format in either a synchronous or asynchronous manner.

References

Brewer, E. W. (1997). *13 proven ways to get your message across: The essential reference for teachers, trainers, presenters, and speakers.* Thousand Oaks, CA: Corwin.

Dienstfrey, S. (1991). *Creative approaches to teaching Shakespeare in high school.* (ERIC Document Reproduction Service No. ED 331 096)

Hungerford, H. (1989). *A prototype environmental education curriculum for the middle school. A discussion guide for the Unesco training seminars on environmental education* (Environmental Education Series 29). Paris: United Nations Educational, Scientific and Cultural Organization, Division of Science, Technical and Environmental Education.(ERIC Document Reproduction Service No. ED 326 420)

Instructional Improvement Committee. (1992). *Instructional improvement handbook.* Wisconsin University Task Force on Establishing a National Clearinghouse of Materials Developed for Teaching Assistant Training. (ERIC Document Reproduction Service No. ED 285 495)

The Panel Planning Sheet

Date:_____Time:_____Site:_____

Intended Audience:

Topic Statement Question:

Objective(s) of the Panel:

Arrangements:

> Setup, Furnishings, Audiovisuals:
>
> Secure Panel Members and Moderator:
>
> Assist With Travel Arrangements:
>
> Obtain Questions From Audience (if this is to be included in the taped format):
>
> Arrange for the Taping:

Pre-Session Meeting:

Tape an Introduction of Panel Members to Audience:

Procedure of Session:

Arrange for Online Interaction (chat, discussion board, etc.) If Included:

Summary Notes:

Post-Session Plans (thank you, etc.):

The Panel Evaluation Sheet
(✱You may wish to have someone else consider these items, as
well as evaluating yourself.)

✱ Was the topic/question well stated? __Yes __No (Explain)

✱ Did travel arrangements run smoothly for all panel members and the
moderator? __Yes __No (Explain)

Were site arrangments adequate? __Yes __No (Explain)

✱ Did the pre-session contribute to the overall effectiveness of the
session? __Yes __No (Explain)

✱ Was the moderator effective in keeping the discussion on track?

. . . in developing cohesiveness?

. . . in clarifying?

__Yes __No (Explain)

✱ What was the quality of panel members' contributions to the
discussion?

✱ Did the summary bring effective closure to the session?
__Yes __No (Explain)

Was there audience participation in the form of questions or comments?
__Yes __No

If so, how did that contribute to the overall effectiveness of the
session?

✱ Which aspect of the session was best?

✱ Suggestions for improvement:

PART III

INTERACTION METHODS

CHAPTER 8
INTERACTION METHOD: GROUP DISCUSSION

CHAPTER 9
INTERACTION METHOD: QUESTIONING

CHAPTER 8
INTERACTION METHOD: GROUP DISCUSSION

Definition

Group discussion is a method of interaction that allows for the interchange of ideas within a context presented by the facilitating instructor. A group discussion follows democratic guidelines and allows everyone to contribute many ideas for others to discuss and reflect upon.

Introduction

Whenever groups of people congregate in the same place, they will talk with one another. It is human nature to be curious about our surroundings and about other people, and the best way to find answers to our questions is to talk with one another. These discussions in a computer environment may be synchronous chats or asynchronous discussion boards. In all cases, a discussion may be information based, concentrating on facts, or it may focus on personal opinions and feelings. People enjoy discussions and the arenas of thought they uncover. One thing quite different about online discussions is that one tends to hear from everyone, even the quiet participant in a class-room setting. Online, this person may very well be the most open in a discussion in which he or she does not have to compete for the floor with more dominant participants.

New ideas can be evaluated and tested using the discussion method. Groups, under the guidance of an instructor, discuss issues to achieve understanding and consensus after much consideration of the viewpoints and ideas presented. Discussions spark new thought and concept exploration, encourage analysis of factual information, and develop open-mindedness toward new attitudes and beliefs.

Group discussions serve intellectual, emotional, and social purposes. Intellectually, discussion helps participants become aware of a diversity of opinions on an issue. It also allows participants to realize the complexity of issues, because they may walk away from a discussion with more questions than when they went into the discussion. This is good because it helps them to think about all the possibilities. Participants must discern the difference between fact and opinion and thus they must practice the skill of listening and analyzing what they hear. Listening also helps them to think out the relevance and application of ideas and content. By sharing these ideas, "Learning can take place on higher intellectual levels (specifically analysis, synthesis, and evaluation) than is possible solely with the recall of information" (Kemp, Morrison, & Ross, 1998, p. 154). Students add personal experiences and weigh how new ideas fit into their experiences in life and work. The small-group response in Figure 8.1 to a streamed video presentation is a reflection on the content followed by a personal experience reflection and challenge.

Emotionally, the participants may have some sort of personal involvement in the issue they are discussing, making it important to them. Others should be sensitive to this. Participants want others to realize that their opinions matter, and once the group responds to this, each participant retains a feeling of self-worth. This is an important

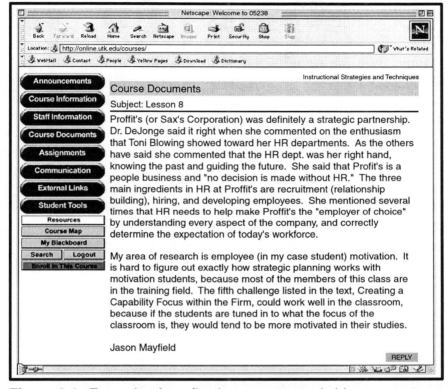

Figure 8.1. Example of a reflection on streamed video presentation followed by a personal experience.

affective quality that is key to the building of self-confidence and a sense of belonging.

Socially, group discussion builds a sense of cohesion and trust with one another. In discussions, differences in opinion, race, gender, and participation should be accepted and celebrated. Differences allow for the diffusion of new ideas and attitudes. Any group work of any sort helps participants build their interpersonal skills and confidence about offering individual opinions in a group setting.

A well-conducted group discussion will end in acceptance of different opinions, respect for well-supported beliefs, and improved problem-solving skills. Overall, it will promote the sharing of information, and all members will gain insight concerning the thoughts of others before reaching consensus on a topic. Bellon, Bellon, and Blank (1992) believe participants in small groups concentrate on the topic at hand due to the support of their peers and individual motivation. Henson (1993) notes that small-group discussions allow participants to get to know each other on a personal level and give them a sense of belonging to a team.

Main Procedural Steps in Using Group Discussion

The purpose of the group discussion is to contribute and circulate information on a particular topic, to analyze and evaluate the information for supported evidence, and to reach an agreement on general conclusions. To do this, several steps must be taken when conducting group discussions.

Step 1—Introduction

The instructor must prepare before the discussion for it to be successful. The instructor should try to introduce a topic on which all of the participants have some background knowledge so they have a basis for discussion. This is why the discussion often follows a lecture or one of the content delivery methods. Once the participants have new information to think about, they are ready for the instructor to stimulate this thinking through a directed discussion. If the participants have experience in the area of discussion, they are also engaging in trying out the new information with the reality of personal experiences and sharing these among group members. The introduction should have four parts.

1. *Instructional objective.* An instructional objective should be given to the participants at the beginning of the discussion.
2. *Purpose.* The instructor should explain why the groups will be discussing the chosen topic.
3. *Relationship.* The instructor must explain how this information fits in with what has already been learned or with what will be learned in the future.

4. *Advanced organizer.* An advanced organizer is some sort of attention grabber that attracts participants' interest. Many discussion topics fail because participants are not drawn into the discussion at the beginning.

The instructor must determine the type of online discussion that will work best for the material and learning objective(s). First, determine the size of the group. There are times when a great diversity of responses will generate the best environment. When this is the case, using a large-group discussion board may work best. When it is important that an entire class see the ideas of each student, let them post their responses and then have the opportunity for commenting on the responses of others.

If the discussion requires a great deal of exchange of ideas and a product of group work, groups of 5 to 8 will be more effective than larger groups. The next decision concerns the **type of online discussion.** The instructor may form groups based upon student's similar interests for further study in that area. For some topics, diversity of student experiences and interests will aid the discussion purpose. Many course management systems have discussion boards that can be formulated for an entire group or for small groups that you select from the class roll. The groups may then select a board where messages and responses can be posted or a chat for synchronous communication. Figure 8.2 shows a small-group page with the options of tools they may use for communication including a discussion board, virtual chat, file exchange, and e-mail. All encourage easy interchange of ideas for group discussions.

Many times when groups are formed and have been working together, the instructor can leave the type up to the group. As the instructor, you can ask to be informed of the times of the chat or you can schedule them for each group at times when you are available. The instructor should be aware that not all technical aspects of discussion boards are alike. Some allow viewing of the responses in a continuous format whereas others follow a threading and individual message–opening format. Make sure students understand the process for not only posting but also reading others' responses so the interaction does indeed take place.

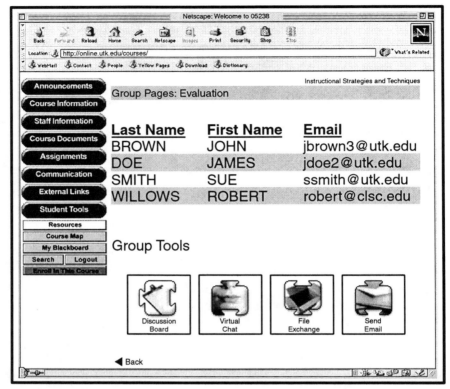

Figure 8.2. Example of a small-group page with options of tools they may use for communiction.

Course management systems often have brief student home pages incorporated into them. They enable all students to introduce themselves to the class, and they may include a picture. Encourage groups to get to know their members by visiting these pages before group work begins. Filling in the template for a student home page, as shown in Figure 8.3, is usually one of the first assignments.

Step 2—Directing the Discussion

Questions usually start the discussion, and the instructor is in charge of starting the discussion. Brookfield (1990) suggests choosing topics that are not too fact oriented or lacking in controversy to spark creative thought and diverse responses. Another way to begin

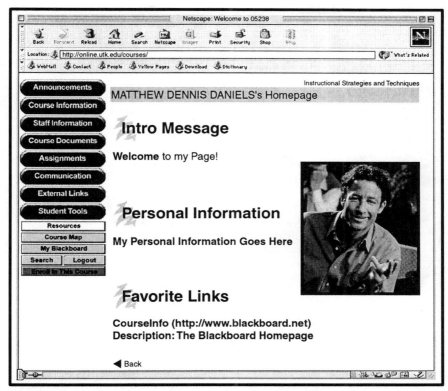

Figure 8.3. Example of filling in the template for a student home page.

the discussion is to ask participants to recall and share personal events that have happened in their lives that relate to the topic. This is a good way to get everyone involved. Questions are excellent motivators for discussion. In Figure 8.4, the instructor is asking that personal experiences be posted in the discussion board and follows with further questions to be sure the students understand the expectations.

Sometimes participants take different thought paths and deviate from the instructional objective, so the instructor might have to reroute the thinking. Leading questions from the instructor can direct participants back to the topic. This means monitoring the small-group discussion boards or chats and adding directing and encouraging comments.

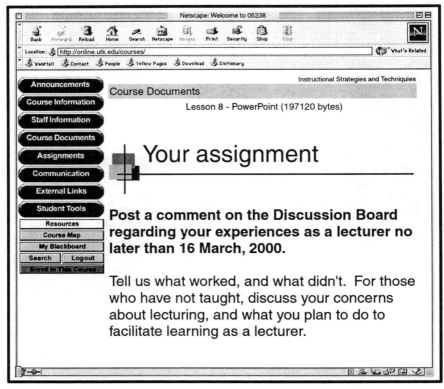

Figure 8.4. Example of a request for personal experiences for the discussion board.

Questions should be worded to avoid yes-or-no responses. They should contain key words and relate to the objective of the discussion. These guided questions will be a model for participants to ask of the peers in their group. King and Rosenshine (1993) found that participants who ask thought-provoking questions in small-group discussions encourage creative answers that increase the learning potential for all.

Once the discussion begins, each participant is expected to add their comments and the discussion board records those responses accurately. The instructor can determine whether all are participating and the quality of the responses. What is added to the discussion is easily available for grading. The student who may be very quiet in a classroom setting now has the floor at his or her leisure on a discussion board, and the richness of the contributions of all usually increases.

As the instructor looks in on the discussion, he or she should decide whether or not participants are spending too much time on insignificant points. However, the instructor should avoid controlling the discussion and should try to enter in only when necessary.

Step 3—Summarizing the Discussion

Summarizing is important to keep participants from being confused or retaining a wrong idea as right. Also for small-group discussions seeking consensus, it is important to summarize the conclusions of all the groups. When asynchronous discussions are used, the summary can be handled in several ways. The instructor may go into each small-group discussion board and add comments of approval or redirection in summary form. Another method is to place in a general area such as "announcements" a summary of the points that were expected to be a part of the discussion. This way participants can self-check the work and review the essence of the objectives for the lesson. Another technique is to select one group's conclusions and post them as a good example. One caution here is to make sure the instructor selects different groups throughout the course.

Variations of Group Discussion

Cooperative Learning Groups

In cooperative learning, a small group of participants works together to achieve a common goal. Cooperative learning operates on the premise that achievement increases as participants work together. Three concepts are incorporated into cooperative learning groups: (a) group rewards, (b) individual accountability, and (c) equal opportunity for success (Slavin, 1994). This type of group work involves careful planning from the instructor. The goals of cooperative learning are (a) positive interdependence and interaction among participants, (b) individual accountability within the group, and (c) interpersonal and small-group skills. This teaching method fosters cognitive development in the areas of retention and achievement and affective development through socialization and self-esteem. Kemp et al. (1998, p. 156) offer helpful guidelines for successful cooperative learning experiences:

- ✗ Limit group size to 3 to 5 students.
- ✗ Compose heterogeneous groups in ability level, gender, and ethnicity.
- ✗ Carefully plan task, materials, and time frame for each activity.
- ✗ Establish some recognition or other reward to motivate groups.
- ✗ Ensure that everyone in the group has a specific task.
- ✗ Use cooperative learning as a supplement for review, practice, remediation, or enrichment.
- ✗ Monitor and assist the groups as needed.
- ✗ Base grades as much as possible on individual group members' personal contributions or achievement. Use group rewards to recognize groups' success.

Problem-Solving Groups

The purpose of the problem-solving groups is to approach real-life problems with an appropriate strategy. These groups are useful to foster cooperation, discovery, inquiry, and critical thinking. For example, several participants might work together to solve mathematical problems through exploration. The participants find many approaches to a problem and test them for the best possible solution. Cooper (1990) states that problem-solving groups help participants come to logical solutions and make responsible decisions.

Group Investigation

The presenter divides participants into small groups based on particular interests. Each group has a designated category, and each gathers information and analyzes it. Participants then prepare and make a presentation to the class about what they discovered. The process teaches participants to work together, to listen to one another, and to support each one's work and opinions. This is a group skill-building teaching method that strengthens peer interaction.

Brainstorming

Brainstorming is a freewheeling session used to solicit ideas or to look for solutions to problems. It is a good change of pace for online discussions. In the first part of brainstorming, the group is concerned only with quantity. A definite time limitation should be placed on this part. It could be 1 or 2 days, but it should be understood that freewheeling ideas will be cut off after that time. Then the group directs its attention to objective judgment of the ideas presented. Hirokawa (1990) suggests that the pooling in a collective manner of information by individuals in a group helps determine the difference between viable and impossible alternatives and ultimately leads to effective communication and decision making.

Brainstorming sessions must first begin with a specific topic or problem. The topic is usually best phrased as a question and should be narrow enough in scope to encourage specific ideas and not broad generalizations.

The teacher or leader should carefully explain how to brainstorm and set the ground rules for the brainstorming session as follows:

- ✗ Submit only one idea at a time or a clear list of ideas in one posting.

- ✗ All ideas are welcomed as long so they pertain to the topic or problem under discussion.

- ✗ Evaluation and criticism are not allowed in Phase 1.

- ✗ Judgment of ideas is postponed until a later time.

- ✗ "Hitchhiking" on other people's ideas is encouraged, especially if it offers a new slant on the original idea and adds creativity.

✗ "It won't work" statements are not allowed.

✗ Quantity is valued. The more ideas offered, no matter how wild, the better.

At the end of the allowed time, the entire list can be screened by the brainstorming group and posted for the whole group to work on. The methods for online screening will require that one participant become caretaker for summarizing the screening and following the instructor's directions for the next steps. The instructor should provide criteria for screening. One way to screen ideas is to divide the ideas by

✗ Ideas most likely to succeed

✗ Best ideas for short range

✗ Best ideas for long range

✗ Ideas that can be pretested before adoption

Advantages, Disadvantages, and Limitations of Group Discussion

When using group discussion, the instructor should be aware of the following advantages, disadvantages, and limitations of this instructional strategy (Brewer, 1997).

Advantages of Group Discussion

1. All participants are expected to contribute, unlike in a classroom when time may limit full participation.

2. It is a good way to get participants interested in a topic.

3. Participants may more easily understand another participant's explanation than the instructor's explanation.

4. The instructor can identify participants who need assistance.

5. The instructor can identify individual opinions about the topic.

6. This method helps participants see relationships among

ideas or concepts related to the topic at hand. (U. S. Professional Teacher Training, 1983)

Disadvantages of Group Discussion

1. It is time-consuming for the participant and for the instructor to monitor.
2. Some participants in the group may make long and involved contributions.
3. It involves less instructor involvement for preparation but more for monitoring than other methods.
4. The discussion can easily get offtrack.

Limitations of Group Discussion

1. It is not a method that transmits information or facts.
2. The discussion must be carefully planned, not impulsive, to be effective.

Summary

Group discussion develops cognitive and affective abilities. It is a process of freely sharing information and insights among peers in a welcoming environment under the guidance of an instructor. Individual effort is encouraged to make a strong team with creative ideas. Meloth and Deering (1994) note that groups are likely to devote a collective effort toward their prescribed task and to become more focused on their goal when working in cooperative groups.

References

Bellon, J., Bellon, E., & Blank, M. (1992). *Teaching from a research knowledge base.* New York: Merrill.

Brewer, E. W. (1997). *13 proven ways to get your message across: The essential reference for teachers, trainers, presenters, and speakers.* Thousand Oaks, CA: Corwin.

Brookfield, S. (1990). *The skillful teacher.* San Francisco: Jossey-Bass.

Cooper, J. (1990). *Classroom teaching skills.* Toronto, Canada: D. C. Heath.

Henson, K. (1993). *Methods and strategies for teaching in secondary and middle schools.* New York: Longman.

Hirokawa, R. Y. (1990). The role of communication in group decision-making efficacy. *Small Group Research, 21*(2), 190-204.

Kemp, J. E., Morrison, G. R., & Ross, S. M. (1998). *Designing effective instruction.* Upper Saddle River, NJ: Prentice Hall.

King, A., & Rosenshine, B. (1993). Effects of guided cooperative questioning on children's knowledge construction. *Journal of Experimental Education, 6*(2), 127-147.

Meloth, M., & Deering, P. (1994). Task talk and task awareness under different cooperative learning conditions. *American Educational Research Journal, 31*(1), 138-165.

Slavin, R. E. (1994). *Cooperative learning: Theory, research, and pratice* (2nd ed.). Boston: Allyn & Bacon.

U. S. Professional Teacher Training. (1983). *Unit 2: Facilitate learning; PAK 5: Conduct a small group discussion.* (General Organization for Technical Education and Vocational Training). Riyadh, Kingdom of Saudi Arabia: Author.

The Group Discussion Planning Sheet

Date:_____Time:_____Site:_____

Purpose Statement:

Specific Topic/Question to Be Discussed:

Relationship to Former/Future Learning:

Advanced Organizer:

Directions for Organizing Groups:

Directions for Discussion:

Plan for Sharing With Entire Assembly:

Handouts (if any):

Equipment (if any):

Summary Notes:

The Group Discussion Evaluation Sheet

(✱You may wish to have someone else consider these items,
as well as evaluating yourself.)

✱ Was the purpose stated clearly? __Yes __No (Explain)

✱ Was there a clear relationship to former/future learning?
__Yes __No (Explain)

✱ How well did the advanced organizer engage participants?

Was the specific topic/question a natural outgrowth of the advanced organizer?

✱ Was the topic appropriate for these participants?
__Yes __No (Explain)

✱ Were directions clear and logical? __Yes __No (Explain)

✱ How well did the facilitator manage any tendency to stray from the topic? __Yes __No (Explain)

Was there a sharing of information with the entire assembly?
__Yes __No (Explain)

✱ Did this contribute to general understanding?
__Yes __No (Explain)

✱ Did the summary clarify and bring effective closure to the activity? __Yes __No (Explain)

✱ What was the most effective aspect of this learning session?

✱ Suggestions for improvement:

CHAPTER 9

INTERACTION METHOD: QUESTIONING

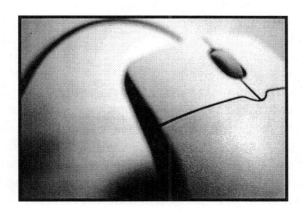

Definition

The questioning method includes presenter-led and participant-led questioning. Questioning may focus on finding a single factual answer or on solving physical, behavioral, philosophical, and historical problems. This method uses the *what, why,* and *how* of inquiry. This method also affords generation of a verbal response from a participant, allowing the presenter to determine what the participant has learned. It is a way to discover and interpret information. Effective questioning encourages participants to think critically and provides feedback to the presenter about participants' understanding.

Introduction

In *presenter-led questioning,* participants practice revealing their ideas to the presenter and to their peers. Ideas shared among participants add variety and knowledge to the class. Questions may be directed to one person, a small group, or a large group. The questioning method provides excellent training for communicating well in a future job. If the presenter asks questions in logical order, participants can be stimulated to think logically. It is important to help participants learn to think in different ways. Participants will stay alert and interested when questions require them to do more than just remember.

With *participant-led questioning*, participants are encouraged to use a scientific approach and to interpret responses to form their answers or opinions. Inquiry is concerned with problem solving, but it does not require solutions. The approach to solving problems is systematic yet flexible, and often there is no one correct answer. Henson (1993) supports the inquiry method because it shuns one correct answer in favor of many ideas and removes fear of failure on the part of the participant when contributing to the exercise. This form of questioning is frequently used in science and math, where participants are "rediscovering" the answer to the problem. The method is, however, relevant for most subjects, including those that address questions of philosophy and behavior that may have no one correct answer.

Use of the questioning method in an online environment generally appears in the form of text embedded within instructional communication venues such as a discussion board, large- or small-group discussion pages, or as accompaniments within text supportive of other instructional methods such as lecture or demonstration.

Main Procedural Steps in Using *Presenter-Led* Questioning

When using the *presenter-led questioning*, the presenter must decide which type of strategy to use. All should have common objectives. Questioning proves most effective when used to

✗ Introduce, summarize, or review a competency

✗ Clarify previous points

✗ Promote understanding

✗ Help participants use ideas as well as remember them

✗ Provide presenters with feedback on participants' learning

Types of *Presenter-Led* Questions

Two types of questions are frequently asked and used as an interaction method by presenters—narrow and broad.

Narrow Questions. These questions, sometimes referred to as *skinny questions*, require little imaginative or deep thinking. They ask for factual information and responses that are predictable. The answers are specific, so the participant either knows them or does not know them. Presenters generally use this method of questioning when drilling or testing reading comprehension. Narrow questions provide a way of going over facts and reviewing for basic understanding. This method should be used to make a transition from lower levels of thinking to higher cognitive levels.

Broad Questions. Broad, commonly called *fat questions*, command a plethora of different possible responses. Thus, responses to this type of question are not predictable. The questions are purposefully thoughtful to promote critical thinking on behalf of the participant. The participant will most likely respond with answers that convey judgment, feelings, or opinions. Broad questions are used to encourage participants to experiment with their options and analyze consequences. These are especially helpful with problem-solving situations. Independent thinking and creativity are expressed as participants move beyond basic recall to evaluative thinking. Figure 9.1 depicts a broad question posed by an instructor in a lesson posted within a course management system.

Both of these questioning strategies are helpful when used at the appropriate time. But first, the presenter should know how to question his or her participants in a way that will be beneficial to both. The procedure for questioning involves five steps: (a) planning questions, (b) asking questions, (c) handling partially correct and completely

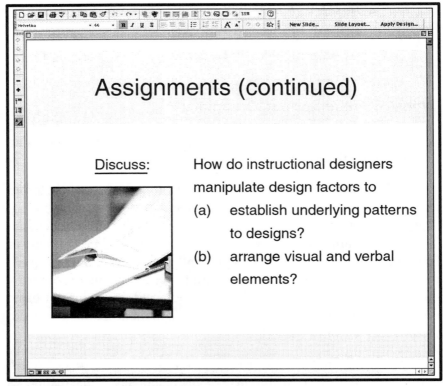

Figure 9.1. Example of presenter-led questioning.

correct answers, (d) handling incorrect answers, and (e) handling no answer at all.

Step 1—Planning Questions

Presenters should carefully plan questions, because poor questions do not help participants learn. Presenters should know how to plan and use good questions. According to Cheek (1989), instructors should use questions to (a) review or summarize lessons, (b) assess what participants know prior to learning new content, (c) promote understanding, and (d) make participants think. He further suggests that instructors should attempt to emphasize important and factual information that is being taught and provide feedback during and after material is presented. The following should be kept in mind when planning questions:

✗ Make questions short enough for the participants to remember.

✗ Include only one idea for each question.

✗ State the question using language familiar to the participant.

✗ Word questions so as to require participants to answer more than "Yes" or "No."

✗ Use questions that are related to the material being learned.

✗ State the question in such a way that the answer is not suggested.

✗ Avoid repeating questions in several different forms. Choose clear wording and remain consistent.

✗ Ask questions in a logical sequence.

✗ Design questions to measure understanding of the subject. Avoid trick questions.

Step 2—Asking Questions

A presenter should begin with a planned set of questions related to a specific objective. The session should then be conducted in the following way. First, ask a question of the group. Next, wait to allow participants to think of their own answers. Finally, call on a participant by name and give that participant time to answer. When asking oral questions, do the following:

✗ Direct questions to an individual within the entire group to initiate a single participant response, as opposed to many talking at once.

✗ Ask different participants in a small group so that each has a chance to participate.

✗ Reward correct answers with positive responses such as "That's right" or "Good," but never discourage a participant who gives an incorrect answer. This leads to embarrassment and withdrawal.

✗ Do not repeat answers given by participants or deliver lectures on ideas introduced by participants.

✗ Call on participants in random order to promote attention by all participants.

✗ Encourage participants to go beyond their first answer. Help them to expand on an idea and to support their response with facts.

✗ Bring other participants into the discussion by asking them to react to another participant's answer.

✗ Allow a wait time of 3 to 5 seconds after asking a question before requesting participant response. Buttery and Michalak (1978) agree that wait time allows participants to think about their answers and helps them to participate more readily, eliminating ineffectual rapid-fire method of questioning.

Step 3—Handling Partially Correct Answers and Completely Correct Answers

When a participant's answer is partially correct,

✗ Give credit for the correct part.

✗ Work with the participant to improve the answer.

✗ Ask another participant to add to the response.

If a participant's answer is totally correct, reward the participant with praise such as "Very good" or "That's correct." Praise encourages participants' participation and provides positive reinforcement.

Step 4—Handling Incorrect Answers

When incorrect answers are given, a presenter should try to remain noncritical in his or her response. Some suggestions are as follows:

✗ Commend the participant for his or her effort, but point out that the main idea was overlooked.

✗ Ask the participant other questions to direct thinking back to the topic and help the participant come to the correct answer.

✗ Tell the participant to think about the question and that you will return to him or her for another try.

Step 5—Handling No Answer at All

It is important for a presenter to remember to never make a participant feel dumb, because he or she will be less likely to participate in future question-answer sessions. All honest answers should be accepted and used to develop further meaning. If a participant cannot answer the question,

✗ Ask another participant.

✗ Try rewording the question in simpler language.

✗ Reteach the material.

Main Procedural Steps in Using *Participant-Led* Questioning

The participant-led questioning method is also known as the inquiry method. It requires that presenters have expertise not only in the subject matter but also in the teaching strategy itself. There are some pitfalls to questioning, and this expertise is necessary to avoid them. In implementing the questioning method, the teacher creates the situation, whether it be physical or psychological. Scientific laws and laws of nature are good examples of physical problems for which truth can be rediscovered with the inquiry method. Problems of ethics and moral decisions in which individual prejudices become an issue are good philosophical problems for inquiry.

Once the problem is presented, the presenter then acts simply as a facilitator. In solving the problem, the participant uses raw data and discipline to address the problem. Once the presenter has set the stage, he or she acts as a structural referee and should refrain from commenting on the direction the discussion is going. For philosophical or ethical inquiry, when participants have gained enough information to develop a hypothesis, the presenter may provide some additional information that challenges that hypothesis, thereby not allowing any answer to be absolute or final.

When the inquiry, or participant-led questioning/discussion has been completed, the teacher should lead the group in reviewing and evaluating the experience, because the process involved is as much a learning experience as the answers given. Bellon, Bellon, and Blank (1992) state that presenters should ask questions that are open ended and exploratory to stimulate participants to examine many options. Participants should be able to share their discoveries, including what aspects of the discussion made them uncomfortable, what turned them off to the whole issue, and whether they felt in tune with the group.

Participant-led questioning should be used only when the leader has enough expertise in the subject matter to handle unexpected "discoveries." Setting up the discovery requires detailed and thorough planning, as well as being sure that proper materials, information, and raw data are available. Inquiry is a method in which the students find the answer themselves. Presenters should be prepared to accept their answers. Brewer (1997) believes participants are able to contribute more critical-thinking skills and to gain more from the learning experience when the atmosphere is one that is more participant oriented and less presenter directed.

Variations of the *Presenter-Led* Questioning Method

Within the main types of *presenter-led questions*, narrow and broad, there are four subtypes. Within narrow questions there are cognitive-memory and convergent. Broad questions can be broken down into divergent and evaluative.

Cognitive-Memory

Cognitive-memory questions are narrow and require basic thinking. They are easily answered with facts, definitions, and memorized material. Often, a one-word answer is sufficient. Houston (1983) argues that this method is individualistic, ignoring the needs of a group, and lacks direction on the part of the presenter and participant.

Convergent

Convergent questions are less narrow than cognitive-memory questions because the participant must put a cluster of facts together to form a basic idea. They demand an explanation, usually about the relationship between two concepts. These questions generally begin with "how" or "why" to elicit the best response.

Divergent

Divergent questions are broad in nature and ask a participant to predict, hypothesize, or infer when responding. A high level of thinking must be used by the student to examine his or her choices and present many acceptable, feasible responses. This method leads to creative thinking and interest in the subject matter and is helpful in problem solving.

Evaluative

Evaluative questions represent the highest level of broad questions. The cognitive levels of the cognitive-memory, convergent, and divergent question methods are meshed together to help organize knowledge in order for the participant to answer with a response that judges, justifies a choice, or defends a particular stance. Evidence must reinforce the selected choice. This method fosters independent, evaluative thinking. Arnold, Atwood, and Rogers (1973) concur that questions that go beyond rote memorization help students process information at higher cognitive levels, thus proving more advantageous for the participant. However, Sampson, Strykowski, Weinstein, and Walberg (1987) offer evidence that there are no conclusive empirical data that link high-level cognitive questioning with academic achievement.

Appropriate Uses

Presenter-led questions may be the best way to begin the process of communication, stimulate thinking, and gain information. Questions allow people to formulate solutions to problems, using collective or individual thought. Responses provide insight into how individuals think and process information, what their personality and interests are, and how they might practically apply what has been learned. Questioning is often used for

✗ Giving directions

✗ Managing an environment

✗ Initating instruction

✗ Creating learning situations

✗ Evaluating learning

✗ Stimulating thinking

✗ Developing attitudes and feelings

✗ Creating interest and motivation

✗ Developing or achieving insight and new possibilities.

There are four types of questioning strategies that presenters should be cautioned against.

Yes **or** *No* **Responses.** The *first* caution regards questioning that yields "Yes" or "No" responses. These answers require little thought on the part of the participant. Unfortunately, it is an easy, quick strategy for the presenter. Participants can easily guess, and they do not have to show supporting evidence for their answers. It is not a strategy that measures how much a participant has learned.

Ambiguous **Questions.** The *second* type of questioning involves asking ambiguous questions. These encourage guessing on the part of the participant because they are not clear to begin with. Participants cannot form meaningful responses to something they do not understand in the first place. These questions may be irrelevant to the lesson and may result in rambling.

Spoon-Fed **Questions.** The *third* caution regards giving too much guidance and leading the student to the presenter's already-chosen "right" answer. The answer is so visible that it is worthless to even ask the question. This strategy encourages participants to be lazy and sloppy in their thinking.

Confusing **Questions.** The *fourth* caution concerns asking confusing questions. These are questions that contain too much material for the participant to grasp at one time. By the time the whole question has been asked, the participant is confused. When faced with "double-barreled" questions, the participant is more concerned with which part to answer first than with critical thinking that offers ideas. Also, presenters sometimes offer unfamiliar vocabulary words or ideas that are above the participants' heads. This leads to frustration among students.

Cheek (1989) suggests that the presenter not ask participants questions that he or she knows participants cannot answer. He further notes that everyone should be given a chance to participate and that a few participants' dominating the class should be avoided.

Questioning strategies should be chosen that appropriately target the level of participants' understanding, the atmosphere of discussion, and the depth of the subject matter. Narrow questions are used for factual drilling, whereas broad questions explore topics in greater depth. A good mix of both, beginning with narrow questions, can lead to a varied lesson that avoids boredom and develops higher order cognitive skills. An effective approach to asking questions is to call on willing and nonwilling volunteers equally to provide each participant with the opportunity to share his or her thoughts. This encourages participation and confidence about opinions.

Instructors are encouraged to use questioning strategies that prompt participants to clarify, correct, or expound on an answer. Begin with narrow questions that orient participants with information that is familiar to them. Then build as they redevelop their answers. Other participants should be encouraged to help struggling students with suggestions on improving their answers. This will not only involve the others but also will take the "spotlight" off the individual participant.

Questioning strategies differ from presenter to presenter, depending on the situation. The presenter must adapt the questioning strategy to his or her participants. Hogg and Wilen (1976) state that if presenters incorporate self-analysis and participant analysis as beneficial feedback when evaluating their questioning style, then students learn more effectively. Question-asking strategies are only successful when they help the presenter achieve objectives and help the participants master learning.

Variations of the *Participant-Led* Questioning Method

In *participant-led questioning, or inquiry*, there is no correct answer. The technique was originated by Socrates and leads to a highly personal experience in learning, even though it is usually approached with a group. The interesting feature of questioning as opposed to most other techniques is that it is a dual learning process. While participants learn about the topic under investigation, they are also learning about the process of questioning. The attitude of learners is important because inquiry is a self-motivating technique.

This method can be used in diverse disciplines and in interdisciplinary learning. It should be used, however, only when cooperation is one of the goals because it fosters cooperation instead of competition. Presenters find they are more participant oriented instead of being subject oriented. This method can enhance small-group inquiry within larger group inquiry. It can be used as a form of simulation. Participants use the data, accept or reject the opinions of others, and arrive at a conclusion collectively. Groups may be asked to study, for example, the heat conductivity in different types of pans by actually conducting experiments and arriving at a conclusion.

Another approach would be to set up a simulation of an ethical question and then get the group to arrive at a conclusion. An example might be a hospital advisory board that has to decide life-or-death questions concerning several patients. In questioning, the presenter provides the materials and the situations, and participants provide the answers or possibilities. Joyce, Weil, and Showers (1992) state that the inquiry method is most successful in promoting critical thinking within an instructional atmosphere when the topic is challenging and somewhat confusing.

Advantages, Disadvantages, and Limitations of *Presenter-Led* Questioning

When using the presenter-led questioning instructional strategy, the presenter should consider the following advantages, disadvantages, and limitations (Brewer, 1997).

Advantages of *Presenter-Led* Questioning

1. It stimulates participant motivation and participation because it involves all participants.
2. It focuses participant attention and develops curiosity.
3. Participants can practice self-expression and gain pride in individual opinion.
4. It adds variety to a lesson.
5. Logically sequenced questions help develop reasoning skills.
6. It reveals individual abilities and interests that enhance the lesson.
7. It can be used to introduce, summarize, review, or clarify.
8. It emphasizes using ideas instead of just memorizing them.
9. It helps participants develop new insights and critical thinking.

Disadvantages of *Presenter-Led* Questioning

1. Shy participants are reluctant to participate.
2. A small group of participants may take over the discussion.
3. Other participants may tune out while the presenter is with an individual participant.

4. If a participant's response is "shot down" by the presenter, the participant may become discouraged and withdraw.

5. Questions may not be phrased in ways that promote critical thinking and interest.

Limitations of *Presenter-Led* Questioning

1. Questions directed at large groups, as well as participants' responses to the question, are sometimes hard to hear.

2. It requires a large amount of class time because of the level of participant involvement.

3. The teacher must provide an open, noncritical environment that welcomes all responses.

4. Too much time may be spent on questions that demand only lower level thinking.

5. Overuse leads to predictability and boredom.

Advantages, Disadvantages, and Limitations of *Participant-Led* Questioning

Considerations for using the inquiry or participant-led questioning method include the following.

Advantages of *Participant-Led* Questioning

1. Participants are actively discovering information. Therefore, retention is high.

2. Participants learn how to follow leads and clues and how to record findings.

3. Motivation comes from within. Participants are intrinsically motivated to participate.

4. It encourages individual and creative thinking.

5. It encourages intuitive thinking.

6. It enables students to discover relationships and cause-effect variables.

7. It is highly participatory.

Disadvantages of *Participant-Led* Questioning

1. The technique is time-consuming.
2. There is lack of textbooks and materials available for presenters.
3. Participants often get bogged down and lose direction before the problem is solved.
4. Participants often discover things other than what was intended to be discovered.
5. An erroneous discovery after great study and effort can be deflating for participants.
6. Presenters must have a strong background in the subject to handle unexpected discoveries.

Limitations of *Participant-Led* Questioning

1. Setting up the problem and conditions requires thorough planning.
2. Proper raw materials and data must be available.
3. Participants' skill level and maturity must be on a level with course objective and subject.
4. It does not stress accumulation of facts.
5. It is best when used with small or medium-size groups.
6. Cooper (1990) notes that the inquiry method is a highly subjective activity, resulting in bias.

Summary

Whether narrow or broad, *presenter-led questioning* sparks intellect and thought when applied to meaningful subject matter. It increases the presenter's awareness of participant comprehension of material and participants' ways of presenting their ideas. When used effectively, it can enhance a lesson and develop interpersonal skills, understanding, and new avenues of thought.

Participant-led questioning is a high-retention, self-motivational style of learning that asks participants not to find the answer that the teacher has in mind but to arrive at their own conclusions and discoveries. It can be used with scientific questions or with emotional and philosophical questions. In some pure forms of inquiry, the assumption is that there is no "right" answer.

References

Arnold, D., Atwood, R., & Rogers, V. (1973). An investigation of relationships among question level, response level and lapse time. *School Science and Mathematics, 7*(3), 591-594.

Bellon, J., Bellon, E., & Blank, M. (1992). *Teaching from a research knowledge base.* New York: Merrill.

Brewer, E. W. (1997). *13 proven ways to get your message across: The essential reference for teachers, trainers, presenters, and speakers.* Thousand Oaks, CA: Corwin.

Buttery, T., & Michalak, D. (1978). Modifying questioning behavior via the teaching clinic process. *Educational Research Quarterly, 3*(2), 46-56.

Cheek, G. (1989). *Basic ideas for electrical instructors.* Washington, DC: National Joint Apprenticeship and Training Committee for the Electrical Industry.

Cooper, J. M. (1990). *Classroom teaching skills.* Toronto, Canada: D. C. Heath.

Henson)cK. T. (1993). *Methods and strategies for teaching in secondary and middle schools.* New York: Longman

Hogg, J., & Wilen, W. (1976). Evaluating teacher's questions: A new dimension in students' assessment of instruction. *Phi Delta Kappan, 58,* 281-282.

Houston, V. (1983). Improving the quality of classroom questions and questioning. *Educational Administration and Supervision, 24,* 17-28.

Joyce, B., Weil, M., & Showers, B. (1992). *Models of teaching.* Boston: Allyn & Bacon.

Sampson, G., Strykowski, B., Weinstein, T., & Walberg, H. (1987).

The effects of teacher questioning levels on student achievement: A quantitative synthesis. *Journal of Educational Research, 80,* 290-295.

The *Presenter-Led* Questioning Planning Sheet

Date:_____ Recommended Viewing/Access Time:_____

Anticipated Composition of Learner Audience:

Topic Statement:

Purpose of Questioning Session:

Relationship to Former/Future Learning:

Directions for Participants:

Methods of Evaluating/Recording Participants' Responses:

     1.
     2.
     3.

Types of Questions to Be Used:

     1.
     2.
     3.

List of Questions:

Summary Notes:

The *Presenter-Led* Questioning Evaluation Sheet

(✱You may wish to have someone else consider
these items, as well as evaluating yourself.)

✱How appropriate were the questions for the participants?
(level of difficulty)

✱Did some of the questions require critical thinking?
__Yes __No (Explain)

Were all participants adequately involved? __Yes __No (Explain)

What reinforcements were used to reward for appropriate responses?

How effectively did the classroom practitioner redirect participants when
responses were inadequate?

How well did the session accomplish the stated purpose?

✱What was the facilitator's level of enthusiasm?

✱What was the general level of interest among participants?

Did the summary serve to clarify any misunderstandings?

Did the summary effectively bring closure to the session?

✱What was best about this session?

Suggestions for improvement:

The *Participant-Led* Questioning Planning Sheet

Date:_____Recommended Viewing/Access Time:_____

Anticipated Composition of the Audience:

Problem Statement:

Objective(s) of Session:

Possible Options:

      1.
      2.
      3.

Resources Needed:

Handouts (background information, process sheet, etc.):

Follow-Up Activity(ies):

Summary Notes (review and evaluation of findings):

The *Participant-Led* Questioning Evaluation Sheet

(✱You may wish to have someone else consider
these items, as well as evaluating yourself.)

✱Was the problem/situation well stated? __Yes __No (Explain)

How well prepared were the participants for this session?

Was the facilitator nonbiased? __Yes __No (Explain)

Was the inquiry process clearly explained? __Yes__No (Explain)

✱How effective was the facilitator in keeping participants focused and moving forward?

✱What was the level of enthusiasm of the facilitator?

✱What was the level of enthusiasm of the inquirers?

How effective were the handouts?

✱Were adequate resources available? __Yes __No (Explain)

✱Were site arrangements adequate? __Yes __No (Explain)

Was time allocation appropriate? __Yes __No (Explain)

How effectively did the participants use the inquiry process to form and defend a hypothesis?

How well did the facilitator direct the inquiry process? (Was he or she helpful without being directive?)

Was summarizing effective in bringing closure and clarifying questions? __Yes __No (Explain)

✱What was best about this learning session?

Suggestions for improvement:

PART IV

APPLICATION METHODS

CHAPTER 10
APPLICATION METHOD: ROLE-PLAYING

CHAPTER 11
APPLICATION METHOD: CASE STUDY

CHAPTER 12
APPLICATION METHOD: SIMULATION

CHAPTER 10
APPLICATION METHOD: ROLE-PLAYING

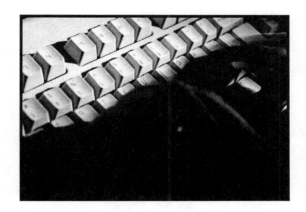

Definition

Role-playing is the spontaneous and open-ended interaction among people in which a problem, situation, or incident is acted out by members of a learning group. In role-playing, actors assume the identity of another person or type of person and react to a situation in the manner that they believe their character would. Role-playing is a type of simulation.

Introduction

Role-playing is a relatively new procedure in adult education and training but is one that children have been perfecting for decades. It is effective in getting people to better understand the emotions and behavior of others in given situations. Role-playing involves using realistic behavior in imaginary situations. In essence, it is "make believe" but the situations and problems are relevant to real life. Because it requires spontaneous reactions on the part of the participants, no script is used. Considerable briefing and preparation on the part of the teacher, however, is essential for success.

Because role-playing captures the interest of the audience as well as of the players, it also provides an excellent opportunity to develop skills in analysis and evaluation. Joyce, Weil, and Showers (1992) state that role-playing (a) examines individual feelings and actions, (b) develops problem-solving techniques to combat social and personal problems, and (c) helps one understand the feelings of others. According to Heinich, Molenda, Russell, and Smaldino (1999), role-playing has proven to be a motivating and effective method of developing socials skills, especially empathy.

Online role-playing may occur using a variety of media and venues ranging from streamed video, streamed audio, links, digital photographs and audio, structured chat, and threaded discussion. For role-playing experiences to be staged properly, learners must know in advance the roles, goals, and responsibilities they will assume. As is the case when using most instructional methods in an online environment, role-playing is generally staged, launched, and wrapped around using written text.

Main Procedural Steps in Using Role-Playing

Before using the role-playing technique, the presenter should evaluate whether it is appropriate for the group of participants. Role-playing is most effective when

✗ The group is small.

✗ The work under study deals with a problem or issue that involves feelings and attitudes rather than straight factual information.

✗ The problem is capable of being solved by the participants.

✗ There is more than one answer to the problem.

There are two kinds of role-playing—structured and spontaneous. **Structured role-playing** involves prewritten cases selected from textbooks, personal experiences, or organizational training material. Structured role-playing usually emphasizes skill development.

Spontaneous role-playing involves no script. It is usually used to help participants gain insight into behavior and attitudes. Hyman (1974) suggests that flexibility and imagination are the major requirements for successful spontaneous role-playing. In an online learning environment, the proposed role-playing scenario is generally staged using text. With structured and spontaneous role-playing, the presenter also has the option of deciding when the role-playing is to be introduced. Some presenters prefer to start with the general and move to the specific, therefore saving the role-playing until the theory discussions and lectures are over.

Other presenters prefer the "discovery" method. In that case, it is good to start with the role-playing exercise. Subsequent discussion would then refer back to the exercise, and group members can be encouraged to develop theories and ideas based on what they have seen. The procedure for implementing role-playing involves six steps: planning, warm-up, implementation, enactment, discussion, and evaluation.

Step 1—Planning

Once the presenter has determined that role-playing is appropriate for the group, the next step is to select the topics. The problems should be carefully defined and should involve conditions that the members of the group will view as real and relevant. The role-playing situation should be typical of problems and conditions that the participants will face, not exaggerated or unrealistic conditions.

Step 2—Warm-Up

Group motivation is important. Especially with adults, the role-playing needs to be something that the group will relate to and not dismiss as preschool silliness. The purpose of the warm-up is to get the group to participate in a constructive manner. The first obstacle to remove is any anxiety members might have about role-playing. Following are several ways of reducing anxiety:

✗ Make the initial role-playing experience one of multiple roles involving three to five members.

✗ Explain carefully to the players what will happen during the role-playing session.

✗ Explain the role-playing process itself.

✗ Swink (1993) encourages the praise of risk taking to build confidence, and the occurrence of mistakes to learn from them.

In spontaneous role-playing, it is sometimes helpful to get the group involved in forming the problem to be discussed. A story or simple plot may be used to introduce the situation. Whenever possible, use volunteers to act out the roles; roles can be selected through chat sessions. Because the audience will be directly involved in the analysis of the role-playing, it is not necessary to force group members who do not want to act to do so.

Two to five players are usually desirable for a single episode. Each character should have a name, and the roles should be discussed in private through e-mail or online chat with each character. Other characters in the episode should not know what their counterparts will be doing or how they will be reacting. When structured role-playing is used instead of spontaneous role-playing, warm-up can include a brief lecture, reading assignment, or multimedia presentation about the topic to be discussed.

Step 3—Implementation

Implementation consists of assigning roles and setting the boundaries for the role-playing. If there is a general instruction sheet of information that all the players and the audience need to know, it should be available online and assigned as advanced reading before the roles are assigned. Once assignments are made via communications such as e-mail, announcement, or discussion postings, players should be given time to read their scripts if it is a structured role-play. If it is a spontaneous role play, a short time can be designated to review the characteristics actors are to portray. Spontaneous role-playing is best suited to online chat.

In spontaneous role-playing, role characteristics should be kept confidential. Neither the other players nor the audience, for example, should know that "Mary's" character description says that she "always finds fault with new ideas." The presenter should distribute online "objective" sheets or inform the audience of relevant things for which to look in role-playing. For example, the presenter may say, "Watch for any techniques that the supervisor uses in dealing with his or her employees." The observer sheets may ask the audience to watch for such details as eye contact, body language, or overt hostility.

Sequentially, the players have had time to review, after which time the leader should introduce each exercise with a brief statement such as "Susan has asked her supervisor, Ernest, for a meeting to discuss a new computer program that she wants to purchase for her division." Then let the enactment begin.

Step 4—Enactment

The true essence of role-playing comes to light in the enactment. Even in structured role-playing, it is the way the players carry out the assignment that enhances the learning technique. Their attitude, interpretation, and presentation are the springboards of the discussion to follow. Keep the enactment moving with as few rules as possible. Exceptions are as follows:

✗ Keep the exercises short—no longer than 10 minutes for spontaneous role-playing and 15 minutes for structured. (Some prewritten, structured role-playing exercises run longer, but those should be considered special cases.)

✗ Stop the role-playing while interest is still high and before too much repetition occurs.

✗ Whenever possible, keep the role-playing going until key participants have had either a chance to respond two or three times or an opportunity to make their positions clear. Note that role-playing accomplished through asynchronous discussion should have predetermined time frames in which responses occur and should include fewer response opportunities in order to avoid loss of interest among participants.

The problems that most often arise during enactment are (a) overacting the role, (b) distorting the facts of the role, or (c) stepping out of the role. Overacting may occur most when a player cops out of participating. In essence, the role player is saying, "If I really exaggerate this, everyone will know that this is not the way I would act normally." If this occurs, the presenter should step in, ask the role player what changes he or she could make to improve the approach, and assess the problem. Sometimes it is helpful to let the audience act as consultants, asking them what the problem is and what approach might be better. Usually the role player will follow the direction the consultants set forth and can continue with the exercise.

Making up facts not in the role generally does not affect the overall results and can usually be left alone. Occasionally, however, the facts may undermine the basic purpose of the role play. In that case, the presenter should stop the exercise or communicate with participants for the purpose of clarifying some of the key facts. The role player should be asked to review the key points and then the exercise can continue. Stepping out of the role requires firm control by the presenter. Simply insist that the player keep in character by saying, "Don't tell us what you would do differently. Just act out the part as if your character were in this situation. Do whatever would be natural."

Step 5—Discussion

It is important to include actors in the role play debriefing discussion, either as part of the audience, before the audience discussion, or as a follow-up to the audience discussion. Discussion should be based on the characters and not on the players. Character names should be used. All discussion should be focused on the facts, problems, and principals and not on an evaluation of the actors' performances. In many cases, it is best to let the actors discuss their feelings about their characters first. This can remove any hesitancy on the part of the audience to discuss certain roles.

In discussion, the presenter should ask questions such as "What happened here?" "How could the situation have been changed?" and "What were the motives and feelings being acted out here?" The presenter should encourage the audience to reach beyond the role play and suggest alternatives and other solutions, then decide on the best one.

Step 6—Evaluation

After the discussion, it is up to the presenter to synthesize all the feelings and facts that have been presented and discussed. The evaluation period is the time to formulate conclusions or solutions to the situations presented. Brookfield (1990) recommends videotaping the role play in order to provide an objective means of critical analysis by which the participants can compare and contrast successes and failures during an evaluation session.

Variations of Role-Playing

Within the two main types of role-playing, structured and spontaneous, there are three subtypes or variations. The variations can be used whether the type of role play is structured or spontaneous, but they occur usually within the structured role play. A true spontaneous role-playing situation obtains both the problem and the solution from the group, and material for the exercise is drawn from them. The three variations are (a) single role plays, (b) multiple role plays, and (c) role rotation. These are addressed in more detail as follows.

Single Role Plays

A single role play involves two or three people acting out roles for a larger group to witness. In an online setting, the single role play transpires via live chat or through small-group discussion posted for others to read. It is then analyzed and discussed by all members of the group. The single role play is especially useful for demonstrating techniques or showing how certain problems can be dealt with.

Multiple Role Plays

A multiple role play involves the whole group as players. The group is broken into subgroups of two or three, and each player is given a written role or a set of characteristics around which to build his or her character. The entire class plays at the same time by way of live chat, and discussion is more effective if done in the small-group settings. Multiple role plays are best used when the group needs practice in dealing with a specific problem or situation rather than changing attitudes or increasing personal insight.

Role Rotation

Online role rotation commonly consists of one person acting out through live chat a problem or situation, followed by several class members responding with solutions. Usually, the discussion can follow after three to five members have responded. It is similar to single role plays but helps to alleviate some of the hesitation players may feel about acting out their roles.

Role-playing strategies can be applied in many situations, and some player characteristics will naturally arise in the situations. Topics such as a businessperson asking his or her boss for a raise, a teacher meeting with an irate parent, an atheist encountering an evangelist, or a Caucasian police officer harressing an African American can all be used for role-playing. Within each role-playing exercise, different roles or types of characters can be presented. (Some players will be given or will assume more than one characteristic.) Examples of some of these are

1. *Information giver,* who contributes his or her beliefs and experiences

2. *Information seeker* who ask questions and brings out principles

3. *Initiator,* who suggests new ideas or new problems

4. *Coordinator,* who tries to bring the group together

5. *Orienter,* who tries to get the group to define the goals

6. *Energizer,* who motivates the group to productivity

7. *Summarizer,* who pulls information together

8. *Encourager,* who offers praise and acceptance

9. *Follower,* who agrees with the majority of the group

10. *Aggressor,* who attacks others' opinions

11. *Recognition seeker,* who relates his own experiences

12. *Distractor,* who interrupts discussion with horseplay or indifference

13. *Blocker* who is negative on all issues and resists the majority at all costs

Advantages, Disadvantages, and Limitations of Role-Playing

Role-playing dramatizes situations. It is commonly used for one of three very different goals: (a) training in specific sales techniques; (b) teaching skills such as interviewing, employee relations, or (c) developing insight into human relations problems and emotions through behaviorally depicting interactions and transactions. Role-playing can best be used to

1. Discover how people might act under certain conditions

2. Gain insight into participants' own feelings and attitudes

3. Encourage understanding of others' feelings and attitudes

4. Illustrate different aspects of a human relations problem and open those aspects for discussion

5. Provide skills and practice in problem solving

Before choosing to use role-playing, the presenter should be sure of his or her objectives. By setting clear-cut targets, presenters are able to use role-playing to its fullest capabilities. If, for example, the objective is to improve skills, then the discussion following the role-playing should focus on how effectively the players used the skills in question. An important point to watch in role-playing is to be certain that the discussion focuses on the character and not the player. By removing the player from the discussion and addressing the character, the risk of hurt feelings is considerably lessened. In discussion, participants should be told to (a) make their comments in relationship to their own feelings, (b) avoid second-guessing, and (c) focus on the role as it was played, not as someone else would have played it.

When using the role-playing instructional strategy, the presenter should be aware of the following advantages, disadvantages, and limitations of this technique (Brewer, 1997).

Advantages of Role-Playing

1. Provides opportunity to practice and develop skills in a safe situation

2. Enables analysis of others' points of view and to express feelings and attitudes

3. Encourages active participation by entire group

4. Addresses behavior and emotions not easily presented in other means

5. Fosters high retention due to dramatic nature of presentation

6. Encourages participants to feel rather than intellectualize a situation

7. Provides means of presenting several solutions to a single problem

8. Encourages creativity and cooperation

9. Provides opportunity to organize thoughts and responses quickly while reacting to a question or situation

10. Individualizes information to participants in a way that is understandable and familiar to them (Span, 1992)

Disadvantages of Role-Playing

1. Some players may feel embarrassed.

2. If players do badly, presenter may have difficulty handling negative comments honestly without harming player.

3. It is time-consuming because it includes not only exercise but follow-up, discussion, and analysis.

4. It is ineffective if exercise runs too long.

5. It can sometimes be above the group's level of understanding.

6. It can overemphasize performance and neglect underlying purpose.

7. Participants with gregarious personalities or acting talent may monopolize the activity.

8. In structured role-playing, role sheets are difficult to design and write.

9. If participants fail to relate to situations, the exercise time is wasted.

Limitations of Role-Playing

1. Participants may be unable to identify realistically with the characters or behaviors.

2. It is not appropriate for large groups.

3. It can become tangential in a hurry.

4. It can be viewed by some as "playing" and not taken seriously.

5. Controversial or highly emotional topics may get out of hand.

6. The method may be harmful to those who lack necessary skills to play (those who are shy or have a speech problem, for example).

7. It may benefit only role players unless the objectives for the class are carefully specified.

Summary

Whether structured or spontaneous, role-playing can fulfill special purposes in the teaching structure. Waters, Woods, and Noel (1992) believe that the presenters play a key role in keeping participants on task during the role play, acting as a resource if questions arise, and helping the participants review and study the worth of their actions during role play. It is helpful in leading participants to better understand their own behavior and the behavior of others. In addition, if properly used and carefully prepared, it can stimulate interesting and thoughtful discussion.

References

Brewer, E. W. (1997). *13 proven ways to get your message across: The essential reference for teachers, trainers, presenters, and speakers.* Thousand Oaks, CA: Corwin.

Brookfield, S. D. (1990). *The skillful teacher.* San Francisco: Jossey-Bass.

Fogarty, R., & Stoehr, J. (1995). *Integrating curriculum with multiple intelligences: Teams, themes, and threads.* Arlington Heights, IL: IRI Skylight Training and Publishing.

Heinich, R., Molenda, M., Russell, J., & Smaldino, S. (1999). *Instructional media and technologies for learning.* Upper Saddle River, NJ: Merrill.

Hyman, R. (1974). *Ways of teaching.* Philadelphia: J. B. Lippincott.

Joyce, B., Weil, M., & Showers, B. (1992). *Models of teaching.* Boston: Allyn & Bacon.

Span, R. (1992). Role play and reactions: Identifying with the elements. *The Science Teacher, 59*(9), 38-40.

Swink, D. F. (1993). Role-play your way to learning. *Training and Development, 47*(5), 91-97.

Waters, E., Woods, P., & Noel, S. (1992). Role play: A versatile cooperative learning activity. *Contemporary Education, 63*(3), 216-218.

The Role-Playing Planning Sheet

Date:_____Recommended Viewing/Access Time:_____

Anticipated Composition of Learner Audience:

Purpose of the Session:

Relationship to Former/Future Learning:

Objective(s) of Session:

Warm-Up Activity:

Directions for Warm-Up:

      1.
      2.
      3.
      4.
      5.

Situations for Role-Play:

Directions for Role-Players:

Directions to Other Participants:

Discussion Questions (to follow each role-playing scenario):

Handouts (for role-players and other participants)

Summary Notes:

The Role-Playing Evaluation Sheet

(✱You may wish to have someone else consider
these items, as well as evaluating yourself.)

How well did the stated purpose relate to former/future learning?

How well did the purpose relate to the role-play situations?

✱Were directions for the warm-up clear and logical?
__Yes __No (Explain)

✱Did the warm-up "set the mood" for the rest of the session?
__Yes __No (Explain)

✱Were the directions to players clear? __Yes __No (Explain)

✱Were the directions to other participants clear?
__Yes __No (Explain)

What did the facilitator do to alleviate any tension regarding
role-playing?

Were the players realistic in their roles? __Yes __No (Explain)

Was there a helpful discussion of each situation? __Yes __No (Explain)

Were the handouts helpful? __Yes __No (Explain)

Did the facilitator effectively summarize and bring closure
to the session? __Yes __ No (Explain)

What was most effective about this session?

Suggestions for improvement:

CHAPTER 11
APPLICATION METHOD: CASE STUDY

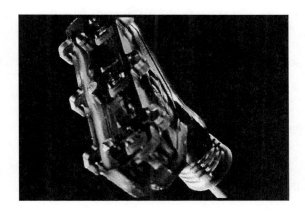

Definition

The case study learning method uses real or hypothetical situations, circumstances, and problems to help participants understand and practice problem solving. The situation, or case, can be either written or in an audio or video format and must contain sufficient detail and data.

Introduction

The case study is a study of firsthand experiences contributed by participants, actual cases pulled by the teacher, or hypothetical cases designed to point out specific problem areas or personality types.

The study of the case is designed to help participants understand and practice problem-solving and decision-making approaches.

Relevant details are studied and examined by the students, who ana-lyze and discuss the problem.

Main Procedural Steps
in Using the Case Study

In the case study method, the process may be accommpolished by the whole group or by subgroups. To begin, the instructor must explain specific guidelines, set objectives, and present a precise means of evaluation. The case should be relevant to students and usually should involve some kind of conflict.

Cases themselves may be presented in one of three ways:

1. The cases may be actual experiences of members of the group. If so, the instructor must to be sure that the partici-pant preparing the experience presents sufficient data for the situation to be reviewed.

2. The case may be written, either factual or hypothetical, and presented to the group by the instructor.

3. The case may be presented by streamed audio or video format. For complicated cases, streaming video is espe-cially helpful because the class can see the behavior of the participants.

A good case or incident should (a) be genuinely interesting and pertinent, (b) be somewhat controversial or at least be open to a difference of opinion, and (c) present events and objective facts from several members of the group. Participants can be given no more information than what the person in the situation received. Proposed solutions should contribute to the overall growth of the participants.

Once the case has been presented, the group work begins by discussion boards and/or chats to identify and interpret the informa-tion as it has been presented. The group then analyzes the data and evaluates the nature of the problem. Whenever possible, data should be objective, with no value judgments prescribed. Analysis of the data is usually by means of reference materials or textbooks but can also include personal interviews, group interviews, or field study.

Participants are invited to share personal feelings and attitudes about the problem, study and evaluate the data, and then make decisions or formulate plans of action.

Christensen (1987) notes that in considering case studies, participants integrate inductive and deductive thinking on the part of the participant to sort through various options, remedy a particular problem, and find the most promising solution.

In some cases, a leader and a recorder may be needed for each group. When using small groups, each group would submit a report. The reports for all groups may be shared with the entire class on an online bulletin board or by whatever format the course management system allows. Comments from the instructor on the ways groups handled the case will allow each member of the class to gain the most from the experience as they look into other groups' work and rethink the issue.

During the discussion phase, the instructor should make sure that the participants are moving in the right direction by providing them with steps to follow for the best results. The following five steps provide good guidelines for the participants to follow:

1. Identify the essential problem.
2. Choose the important facts to be considered with the problem.
3. List several possible solutions.
4. Evaluate the potential results of each solution.
5. Determine which one solution is best.

Variations of the Case Study

The case study has few variations. A large group can be divided into smaller groups who study the problem independently. The class can study the case as a whole, or the cases can be studied and solved on an individual basis.

In addition, the manner in which the case is presented and the time period that is used to work on the case and arrive at a decision can vary. The case can be presented in real time, and the participants can view a live transmission of the problem and work synchronously in small groups or in the large group to solve the case. In other situations, the case can be presented in written or audio/video formats that are available in the course for students to access and work on in their own time frame. A time should be designated for reaching a solution. The time may vary from a week or an entire semester.

Appropriate Uses, Suggestions, and Cautions

The case study method is commonly used when the topics under consideration fall into one of the following categories:

✗ Human relations

✗ Job interviews

✗ Salesmanship, particularly with experienced salespeople

✗ Supervisory training

✗ Business organizational situations

✗ Distribution economics

In addition, the method can be effectively used for any subject of study in which issues are discussed or opinions are apt to be divided.

The case study method is useful for finding solutions to a wide variety of problems and situations. It is not effective when searching for abstract principles. When the participants do not have real experiences to draw on to illustrate the points under study, then case studies can provide an excellent frame of reference. Ryan (1994) insists that the case acts as a catalyst that encourages participants to play the roles of the characters in a situation, allowing them to problem solve from a personal, realistic perspective. It encourages discussion and is good for getting an entire group focused on a specific problem.

The case study technique provides a good forum for exchanging ideas about real-life problems that the students may actually face in the world of work. In doing so, it helps bridge the gap between classroom and real life.

Caution is necessary because the method depends on well-prepared cases and an effective discussion leader. Often, especially when dealing with complex situations, students need to be experienced in handling real-life situations. When presenting the case to be studied, the situation must be clearly and adequately presented with enough details to enable students to get a clear picture of the situation. Owenby (1992) is convinced that case studies must be descriptive, in the form of a story, sequential in order, and realistic for participants to approach them eagerly.

The method requires students to deduce the principles involved, make decisions, and predict results. Maturity of participants is often an issue in deciding whether or not to use the case study method.

Advantages, Disadvantages, and Limitations of the Case Study

According to Brewer (1997), when using the case study instructional strategy, the instructor should consider the following advantages, disadvantages, and limitations of this technique:

Advantages of the Case Study

1. Interest and motivation of participants are generally high.
2. There is better retention of content due to active student involvement.
3. It develops responsibility on the part of the participants.

4. Conclusions are made based on the participants' problem-solving skills, and practice sharpens those skills.

5. Realistic cases bridge the gap between school and the real world.

6. The leader can present a problem in a minimum amount of time, especially if film or other audiovisuals are used to present the case.

7. Boyce, King, and Harris (1993) state that case studies encourage participants to positively critique peers' ideas and to work cooperatively in a group.

Disadvantages of the Case Study

1. It is time-consuming.

2. Good case studies that participants can relate to are hard to find.

3. Instructor must be well prepared for the topic of study.

4. Students may come to believe that all complex problems have simple solutions, based on case study experiences.

5. Cases developed by participants may be controversial and difficult for an instructor to handle.

6. The problem may seem irrelevant to some class members.

Limitations of the Case Study

1. It is most effective when used with mature participants.

2. Resources and materials needed to study cases may not be readily available.

3. Evaluation is difficult and time-consuming due to the open-discussion format of the cases.

4. Cases presented for discussion must be within the experience range of the group.

5. If cases are not presented clearly and with sufficient data, participants may get sidetracked into reading conditions into the case.

Summary

Case studies are based on data and research while drawing from real-life situations. They provide high retention of ideas and high levels of motivation for the participants, especially when the case is one that they can relate to. Case studies provide active student participation. Stolovitch (1990) praises the case study method as an activity that sharpens problem-solving skills. The presenter, once the case is carefully chosen, can also use a wide range of other teaching methods to complement the case study discipline.

References

Boyce, A., King, V., & Harris, B. (1993, March 24-28). *The case study approach for pedagogists.* Paper presented at the annual meeting of the American Alliance for Health, Physical Education, Recreation and Dance, Washington, DC.

Brewer, E. W. (1997). *13 proven ways to get your message across: The essential reference for teachers, trainers, presenters, and speakers.* Thousand Oaks, CA: Corwin.

Christensen, C. R. (1987). *Teaching and the case method.* Boston: Harvard Business School Press.

Owenby, P. H. (1992). Making case studies come alive. *Training, 29*(1), 43-46.

Ryan, C. W. (1994, May 21). *Case studies in teacher education: A series for working with students at risk.* Paper presented at Central State University, Wilberforce, Ohio.

Stolovitch, H. (1990). Case study method. *Performance and Instruction, 29*(9), 35-37.

The Case Study Planning Sheet

Date:_____Time:_____Site:_____

Purpose of the Case Study:

Relationship to Former/Future Learning:

Objective(s) of Session:

By Which Method Will the Case Study Be Presented?

1. Actual experiences that members of the group have had
2. A written case, either factual or hypothetical
3. Case presented by audio or video format

Steps to Take to Carry Out a Case Study:

1. Identify the true problem.
2. Choose the important facts to be considered with the problem.
3. List several possible solutions.
4. Evaluate the results of each solution.
5. Determine which one solution is best.

Discussion Questions (to follow case study):

Handouts (concerning case study and other information
relating to the case):

Summary Notes:

The Case Study Evaluation Sheet
(✱You may wish to have someone else consider these items,
as well as evaluating yourself.)

✱How well did the stated purpose relate to former/future learning?

Was the case study appropriate for the topic? __Yes __No (Explain)

✱Was the method by which the case study was presented appropriate?
  __Yes __No (Explain)

✱Were time allocations suitable? __Yes __No (Explain)

✱Were the directions clear and logical? __Yes __No (Explain)

✱Were the directions to other participants clear?
  __Yes __No (Explain)

What did the facilitator do to alleviate any tension regarding
the case study?

Were the discussion questions that followed the case study appropriate?
__Yes __No (Explain)

✱Were the handouts helpful in presenting the case study?
  __Yes __No (Explain)

✱Did the facilitator effectively summarize and bring closure
  to the session? __Yes __No (Explain)

✱What was most effective about this session?

✱Suggestions for improvement:

CHAPTER 12
APPLICATION METHOD:
SIMULATION

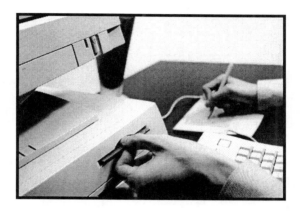

Definition

Simulation, experiment, research and verification, practical exercise, and game represent a collective application method in which teaching and learning occur based upon virtual or simulated practice, research, and investigation. While learning, participants study a basic principle by applying that principle and then observing the results of their applications.

Introduction

The simulated practice is used to clarify information that learners already know or to try to discover unknown information. In the classroom, this collective method, hereinafter referred to as simulation, is most effectively used to verify a basic principle by simulating a potentially real-life experience that will prove or disprove the principle by observing the results. Piskurich and Sanders (1998) report simulation as an increasingly popular learning-intensive instructional method.

Simulation is a way to collect information, classify that information on the basis of the activity, evaluate the information, and then draw conclusions based on what has been seen. Retention rate is high as long as the simulation works. In an online learning environment, the simulation method generally involves use of a series of links through which participants travel; asynchronous text- and graphic-based discussion, exercises, or experiments; or CD-ROM files. These are staged and wrapped around with meticulously written instructions. The following three examples of good simulations appear as URLs:

1. http://medicus.marshall.edu/medicus.htm (accessed June 2000).

2. http://www.cudenver.edu/~mryder/itc_data/net_teach.html (accessed June 2000).

3. http://www.wested.org/tie/dlrn/examples.html (accessed June 2000).

Coleman's study (as cited in Hyman, 1974) reports having delineated five kinds of rules that govern or regulate successful simulations. These include *procedural rules, behavior constraint rules, goal rules, environment response rules*, and *police rules*. These rules are established and communicated to participants prior to starting a simulation. Common simulation characteristics, according to Hyman (1974), include

✗ Possesses clearly focused concepts and processes selected by the presenter as the ones that participants need to consider

✗ Involves participants in simulation of the critical elements of the selected processes based on a valid model

✗ Has an analytical decision model that has the dramatic qualities of a game

✗ Begins with an explicitly prepared scenario and playing directives

✗ Actively involves each participant

✗ Requires participants to assume general rather than specific roles

✗ Starts quickly and lasts a relatively short period of time

✗ Keeps the instructor's own preferences from influencing the simulated practice

Main Procedural Steps in Using Simulation

For a simulation to be an effective teaching tool, it must work. Trying to explain why a simulation fails defeats the purpose of the planned experience and confuses the learner. To help ensure success, the leader or teacher should follow these steps:

1. Make sure the participants understand the learning principle under consideration.

2. Outline in detail the situation involved in the scenario and the steps to be taken in the simulation.

3. If the participants are going to develop their own plan for testing the principle, the leader or teacher should carefully check the plan before they begin.

4. Explain the rules and pattern of engagement in the simulation.

5. Engage the group in the simulation.

6. Require a report on the results of the experiment. This enables the teacher to see if the student observed and confirmed the principle or just "rigged" the experiment to give the expected result.

7. Supplement simulation with other instructional sessions.

8. Encourage students to add refinements to the simulation and introduce refinements as appropriate

9. Halt the simulation when engagement ceases or when time runs out.

10. Hyman (1974) recommends that the simulated experience

follow with a debriefing that allows participants to compare simulated experience with theory and real-life practice.

11. Encourage learners to talk about their beliefs and feelings during the simulation.

12. Encourage learners to talk about the similarity of the experience to the reality.

13. Encourage learners to talk about future activities that can build upon their experience with the simulation.

14. Summarize, generalize, and conclude.

15. Move forward by closing the simulation experience with structure suitable to launch into new activities built upon the simulation experience.

16. Vary the type of simulation used.

In preparing a way to study the results of the simulation, the leader or teacher may need to help the participants set up their charts, graphs, or whatever means they are using to measure results. Check to be sure that these are set up so that insignificant and irrelevant data can be eliminated.

Simulations can be done as a large group, in pairs, in subgroups, or individually. If materials are limited, the leader or teacher can perform the experiment for the whole group while each records his or her own observations.

Variations of the Simulation Method

Experiments, practical exercises, and games can be used to verify and impress on participants the existing laws and principles. This is done not to teach participants the principle, but for the sake of emphasis, retention, and complete understanding. Such simulations can also be used to improve practices or processes by searching for better ways to carry out the procedure. Henson (1993) offers simulation as an experimental way of learning that allows participants to put themselves in hypothetical situations in order to problem solve.

Experiments are often used to verify scientific knowledge. It is not a method that is suitable for presenting skills or discovering scientific laws. Caution should be used in choosing this form of simulation. A failed experiment is a failed lesson. The experimental techniques should be well within the ability of the group and provide results that are conclusive. Principles should be presented before the experiment by other methods, such as lecture. As a teaching method, the experiment should be used to verify, not to discover. Roth (1994) believes that learning through the use of experiments yields experience with "situated learning, total learning environments, self-directed project activity, authentic practice and collaborative learning" (p. 219), which are current practices in education instruction that extend into the workplace.

Many scientific laws can be verified in the classroom with simple experiments. In addition, in teaching shop or other vocational classes, many of the practices used are based on scientific principles, and experiments can be used to verify and emphasize those practices.

Research and verification is another type of simulation. In research, the participants attempt to find a solution to a problem or theory for which no satisfactory answer has yet been found. The research method typically requires mature and trained participants. Sometimes leaders or teachers will attempt to combine the research and verification methods by withholding the knowledge of the principle until after the experiment has been completed. Although the thrill of discovery may be stronger in those situations, so is the percentage of failure. Few students have the degree of imagination and discipline to observe the outcome of the experiment and arrive at the basic principle.

Advantages, Disadvantages, and Limitations of the Simulation Method

When using the simulation instructional strategy, Brewer (1997) noted that the leader or teacher should be aware of the following advantages, disadvantages, and limitations of this technique.

Advantages of the Simulation Method

1. It is excellent for verifying technical information.

2. Hands-on experiments increase retention rate.

3. It calls for analysis and careful observation.

4. It is a good technique to mix with other, less interactive techniques, such as the lecture.

Disadvantages of the Simulation Method

1. It is limited in subject use and most effective in teaching related science.

2. It is not suitable for teaching skills.

3. It requires a base of knowledge of the principle to be studied before simulation begins.

4. Unless carefully chosen and prepared, it can have a high degree of failure, which negates the purpose of the simulation.

Limitations of the Simulation Method

1. The research and verification type of simulation is best for mature, trained participants.

2. Required materials and suitable equipment can be costly.

3. Osborne and Freyberg (1985) state that often experiments are merely controlled demonstrations in which the participant and teacher already know the desired result, leaving no room for experimentation in the truest sense.

Summary

The simulation method is most often used for science, chemistry, physics, or to test principles on which skills are based. In the simulation method, information and principles are presented by other means, then verified by the simulated experience. Based on their observations of the simulation, participants collect the information, classify it, evaluate it, and then make deductions.

References

Brewer, E. W. (1997). *13 proven ways to get your message across: The essential reference for teachers, trainers, presenters, and speakers.* Thousand Oaks, CA: Corwin.

Heinich, R., Molenda, M., Russell, J., & Smaldino, S. (1999). *Instructional media and technologies for learning.* Upper Saddle River, NJ: Merrill..

Henson, K. T. (1993). *Methods and strategies for teaching in secondary and middle schools.* New York: Longman.

Hyman, R. (1974). *Ways of teaching* (2nd ed.). Philadelphia: J. B. Lippincott.

Osborne, R., & Freyberg, P. (1985). *Learning in science.* Hong Kong: Heinemann.

Piskurich, G., & Sanders, E. (1998). *ASTD models for learning technologies, roles, competencies, and outputs.* Alexandria, VA: American Society for Training and Development.

Roth, W. M. (1994). Experimenting in a constructivist high school physics laboratory. *Journal of Research in Science Teaching, 31*(2), 197-223.

The Simulation Planning Sheet

Date:_____Recommended Viewing/Access Time:_____

Title of Simulation:

Purpose of Simulation:

Principles/Concept(s):

Vocabulary:

Procedures and Directions:

Handouts:

Media Needed:

Text-Based Resources Needed:

Summary Notes:

The Simulation Evaluation Sheet

(✱You may wish to have someone else consider
these items, as well as evaluating yourself.)

Was the simulation appropriate for teaching the stated concept?
__Yes   __No (Explain)

Was the simulation designed to be a true investigation?
__Yes   __No (Explain)

Were vocabulary words defined well? __Yes __No (Explain)

✱Did participants appear to have necessary prerequisites
for this lesson? __Yes __No (Explain)

Was the procedure adequately explained before students
began working? __Yes __No (Explain)

Were the handouts helpful? __Yes __No (Explain)

Was there a check for understanding regarding
    a.   basic principles? __Yes __No (Explain)
    b.   vocabulary? __Yes __No (Explain)
    c.   procedure and directions? __Yes __No (Explain)

✱How effectively were participants' questions handled?

Were most participants successful in performing the simulation?
__Yes __No (Explain)

Was there a check for understanding at the end of the session?
__Yes __No (Explain)

Did the classroom practitioner summarize the lesson effectively?
__Yes __No (Explain)

Was the time allocated adequately? __Yes __No (Explain)

What provisions were made for participants who might finish early?

✱How enthusiastic was the classroom practitioner?

✱How much enthusiasm was there among participants?

What aspects of the lesson were most effective?

AUTHOR AND WORD INDEX

CORWIN
PRESS

The Corwin Press logo—a raven striding across an open book—represents the happy union of courage and learning. We are a professional-level publisher of books and journals for K–12 educators, and we are committed to creating and providing resources that embody these qualities. Corwin's motto is "Success for All Learners."